TUTĀNKHAMEN

AMENISM, ATENISM AND EGYPTIAN MONOTHEISM

(Frontispiece.)

PAINTED LIMESTONE HEAD OF A QUEEN IN THE MUSEUM AT BERLIN.
It is supposed to represent Queen Nefertiti, wife of Ȧmenḥetep IV.

TUTĀNKHÅMEN

AMENISM, ATENISM AND EGYPTIAN MONOTHEISM

WITH HIEROGLYPHIC TEXTS OF HYMNS TO ÅMEN AND ÅTEN, TRANSLATIONS AND ILLUSTRATIONS BY

SIR ERNEST A. WALLIS BUDGE, LITT.D., D.LITT.
KEEPER OF THE EGYPTIAN AND ASSYRIAN ANTIQUITIES IN THE BRITISH MUSEUM

BELL PUBLISHING COMPANY
NEW YORK

TO

THE MEMORY OF

GEORGE EDWARD STANHOPE MOLYNEUX HERBERT

EARL OF CARNARVON

Library of Congress Catalog Card Number: 79-160615.

This edition is published by Bell Publishing Company, a division of Crown Publishers, Inc. by arrangement with Arno Press, Inc.

d e f g h

CONTENTS

NOTES

The kings of the XVIIIth dynasty reigned about 230 years, *i.e.*, from about B.C. 1580 to 1350; their names are as follows :—

Åāḥmes 1580, reigned about 22 years.
Åmenḥetep I, about 1558-7, reigned about 10 years.
Thothmes I, about 1546, reigned about 30 years.
Thothmes II, about 1500, reigned about 3 years.
Ḥatshepsut
Thothmes III } about 1500 to 1447.
Åmenḥetep II, about 1448, reigned about 26 years.
Thothmes IV, about 1420, reigned about 8 years.
Åmenḥetep III, about 1412, reigned 36 years.
Åmenḥetep IV, about 1376, reigned 17 years.
Sākarā
Tutānkhåmen } reigned 8–12 years.
Åi
Ḥeremḥeb, about 1350, reigned 34 years.

In the transliterations of proper names a few diacritical marks are used :—å=short *a*, *e*, or *i*; ā=a in father; ḥ is a strongly aspirated h; ṭ=a sound something like d; ḳ, a deep guttural like the Hebrew ק; ʻa=the sound of the Hebrew *ayin*.

ILLUSTRATIONS

1. Plates

2. Illustrations in the Text.

PREFACE

THE announcement made early in December, 1922, of the discovery of the Tomb of Tutānkh-ȧmen in the Valley of the Tombs of the Kings in Western Thebes by the late Lord Carnarvon and Mr. Howard Carter sent a thrill of wonder and expectation through all the civilized peoples on the earth. In the accounts of the contents of the Tomb, which were published with admirable promptness and fullness in The *Times*, we read of bodies of chariots, chairs of state, gilded couches, royal apparel, boxes of trinkets and food and cosmetics and toilet requisites, large bitumenized wooden statues, alabaster vessels of hitherto unknown shapes and beauty, and countless other objects, until the mind reeled in its attempts to imagine the sight that met the eyes of the two discoverers when they entered the two outer chambers. Those who have seen the smaller objects and have enjoyed the privilege of examining them have been amazed at their exquisite beauty and finish; and there is no doubt that the importance of the "find," from an artistic point of view, can be expressed in words only with difficulty. It is easy to believe Sarwat Pasha when he says none of the accounts published have really done justice to the "finds," which, however, is not surprising, since their beauty is unique and indescribable (*Times*, Jan. 18, 1923, p. 9).

All the writers who have described and discussed the discovery have, quite rightly, lost no opportunity of proclaiming the great value and importance of Lord Carnarvon's "find" as illustrating the arts and crafts that were practised in the city of Åakhut-Åten under its founder, the famous Åtenite king, Åmenḥetep IV. But some of them have been led astray by their eagerness to do ample justice to the great discovery, and have introduced into their eulogies statements of a historical character which are incorrect. Some have declared that the information derived from the "find" makes necessary the rewriting and recasting of the history of the XVIIIth dynasty, but there is no foundation for this statement, for the authorized accounts of the Tomb of Tutānkhåmen and its contents include no new historical facts. Lord Carnarvon may have obtained from the tomb information that would amplify our knowledge of the reign of Tutānkhåmen, but if he did so he did not publish it. As matters stand we know no more now about the reign of this king than we did before Lord Carnarvon made his phenomenal discovery. Other writers have tried to make out that Tutānkhåmen was one of the greatest of the kings of Egypt, but this is not the case. When he came to the throne he professed the same religion as his wife, that is to say, the cult of Åten, the Solar Disk, or Atenism, and for a short time he continued to do so. But he soon realized that Atenism had failed, and then he substituted the name of Åmen for Åten in his own name and that of his wife, and became a fervent

follower of Åmen and a worshipper of the old gods of his country. The fame of Tutānkhåmen really rests on the fact that he restored the national worship of Åmen, and made the Atenites to relinquish their hold upon the revenues of this god. Other writers again have tried to show that Tutānkhåmen was the " Pharaoh of the Exodus," and also that it was his wife Ānkh-s-en-pa-Åten (or Åmen) who took Moses out of his ark of bulrushes and brought him up. But there was more than one Exodus, and Tutānkhåmen was not King of Egypt when any of them took place. And strange views have been promulgated even about some of the articles of furniture that Lord Carnarvon found in the tomb. Thus the funerary couch or bier with legs made in the form of a strange beast has been declared to be of Mesopotamian origin ; but such is not the case. The beast represented is the composite monster called " Āmmit," *i.e.* " Eater of the Dead," and she is found in the Judgment Scene in all the great papyri containing the Theban Recension of the Book of the Dead. About her component parts there is no doubt, for in the Papyrus of Hunefer it is written, " Her fore-part is crocodile, her hindquarters are hippopotamus, her middle part lion (or cat)," 
.
The Mesopotamians knew of no such beast, and the couch or bier could only have been made in

Egypt, where the existence of Āmmit was believed in and the fear of her was great.

Some of the writers on Lord Carnarvon's discoveries discussed not only the Tomb of Tutānkhȧmen, but the religious revolution which seems to have been inaugurated by Ȧmenḥetep III, at the instance of his wife Queen Ti, and was certainly carried on with increasing vigour by their son, Ȧmenḥetep IV, who believed that he was an incarnation of Ȧten, the god of the Solar Disk. Their discussions gave many people an entirely false idea of the character of Ȧmenḥetep IV, and of the nature of the cult of Ȧten. This king was described as a reformer, an individualist, and an idealist and a pacifist; but he was a reformer who initiated no permanent reform, an individualist who diverted the revenues of the gods of his country to his own uses, an idealist who followed the cult of the material, and a pacifist who lost Egypt's Asiatic Empire. His "Teaching" proclaimed the "oneness" of Ȧten, which has been compared to the monotheism of Christian nations; but for centuries before his time the priesthoods of Heliopolis, Memphis, Hermopolis and Thebes had proclaimed this self-same oneness to be the chief attribute of their gods. This "Teaching" was said to inculcate a religion and morality superior to any doctrine found in the Old Testament, and some enthusiasts would have us believe that in spiritual conceptions and sublime precepts it surpassed Christ's teaching as set forth in the Gospels. Practically all that we know of the

"Teaching" of Åmenḥetep IV is found in a short hymn, which is attributed to the king himself, and in a longer hymn, which is found in the Tomb of Åi, his disciple and successor, at Tall al-'Amârnah. The language and phrasing of these works are very interesting, for they show a just appreciation of the benefits that man and beast alike derive from the creative and fructifying influence of the heat and light of the sun. But I cannot find in them a single expression that contains any spiritual teaching, or any exhortation to purity of life, or any word of consciousness of sin, or any evidence of belief in a resurrection and a life beyond the grave. It is of course possible that all the religious works of the Atenites, except these hymns, have perished, but the fact remains that it is upon these two hymns, and the extracts from them which are found in the tombs of officials at Tall al-'Amârnah, that modern writers have founded their views and statements about the highly spiritual character of the religion and morality of the Atenites.

Whilst discussing these and similar matters here with Lord Carnarvon about the middle of last December, he suggested that I should put together, in a small book, the known facts about the reign of Tutānkhåmen, and add two or three chapters on the cults of Åmen, Åten, and Egyptian Monotheism, which had been so completely misrepresented. He was particularly anxious that translations of some of the hymns to Åmen and Åten should be given, and that the most important of them should be accompanied by the original hieroglyphic texts, so that those who cared to go into the matter might have the means of forming their own conclusions about the character of the hymns to Åten, and deciding whether it was spiritual or material. In the following pages I have tried to carry out his suggestion, and in the circumstances perhaps it will not be out of place to say a few words about his labours in the field of Egyptian Archaeology.

In the winter of 1907-08, Lord Carnarvon carried out a series of comprehensive excavations at Drah abû'l Naḳḳah and in the Valley of Dêr al-Baḥarî in Western Thebes. In these, as in all his subsequent excavations, he was assisted by Mr. Howard Carter, formerly Inspector in the Service of Antiquities of Egypt. This gentleman possessed very special qualifications for the work that he undertook for Lord Carnarvon, namely, a good knowledge of colloquial Arabic, great experience in dealing with the natives and the "antica" dealers in the country, skill in the practical work of excavation, and keen interest in Egyptian Archaeology. At Dêr al-Baḥarî, Lord Carnarvon discovered two important ostraka inscribed with texts, the one dealing with the deeds of King Kames, and the other containing a portion of a new version of the Precepts of Ptaḥ-ḥetep. In 1908-09 he discovered the tomb of Tetȧki, and a tomb of the XXVth dynasty containing the coffins of nine persons. In 1910-11 he discovered an unfinished temple of Ḥatshepsut, a ruined temple of Rameses IV, a cemetery of the XIIth dynasty, and a number of early burials. A full account of what he did at Thebes will be found in his *Five Years' Explorations at Thebes* (1907-11), Oxford, 1912. This book is illustrated by eighty fine folio plates, and is one of the fullest accounts hitherto published of archaeological work done in Egypt. In 1911-12 he continued his excavations at Thebes, and broke new ground at Xoïs, in the Delta. In 1912 he discovered at Thebes a large temple-deposit of Ḥatshepsut, consisting of alabaster jars, tools, etc., and a number of pit-tombs of the XIIth dynasty. In 1915 he discovered and cleared out the Tomb of Ȧmenḥetep I, and in 1916-17 he discovered a tomb which had been prepared for Ḥatshepsut. The latter contained a magnificent sarcophagus of crystalline limestone inscribed with the Queen's name and titles as wife of the reigning Pharaoh. It is impossible to enumerate here, however briefly, the various excavations which he carried out at Thebes between 1907 and 1921, but it must be stated that he superintended them all personally, and that he alone defrayed all the expenses, which, as will be readily understood, were very considerable.

In recent years he sought for a wider sphere of excavation, and turned his attention to the Valley of the Tombs of the Kings in Western Thebes, which was one of the sites reserved for Government excavation. During the early years of this century Mr. T. Davis obtained permission to dig there from the late Prof. Maspero, Director of the Service of Antiquities of Egypt, and, with the help of Mr. Howard Carter and Mr. Ayrton, he succeeded in locating and excavating the tombs of Queen Ḥatshepsut, Thothmes IV, Ḥeremheb, Menephthah, Saptaḥ, and the unopened tomb of Iuȧu and Tuȧu, the father and mother of Queen Ti. When he had done this he announced to Maspero, "The Valley is now cleared, there are no more royal tombs in it"; and most people were willing to accept these words as the statement of a fact. But Lord Carnarvon did not believe that Mr. Davis's opinion was correct, and, having obtained the necessary permission from the Government, he and Mr. Carter set to work to *prove* that it was not. Each *felt* that somewhere in the Valley one or two royal tombs must still exist, and knowledge, judgment, unceasing labour, and luck enabled them to light upon the most magnificent archaeological "find" ever made in Egypt. The following extract from a letter which he wrote to me on December 1, 1922, shows how he personally regarded his great triumph. He says:—

"One line just to tell you that we have found the most remarkable 'find' that has ever been made, I expect, in Egypt or elsewhere. I have only so far got into two chambers, but there is enough in them to fill most of your rooms at the B.M. (upstairs); and there is a sealed door where goodness knows what there is. It is not only the quantity of the objects, but their exceptional beauty, finish and originality, which makes this such an extraordinary discovery. There is a throne, or chair, there more beautiful than any object that has been found in Egypt; alabaster vases of the most marvellous work, and quite unknown except as represented in the tombs; couches of state, chairs, beds, wonderful beadwork, four chariots encrusted with precious stones, life-size bitumenised figures of the king in solid gold sandals and covered with insignia, boxes innumerable, the king's clothes, a shawabti about 3 feet high, sticks of state. I have not opened the boxes, and don't know what is in them; but there are some papyrus letters, faïence, jewellery, bouquets, candles on ankh candlesticks. All this is in [the] front chamber, besides lots of stuff you can't see. There is then another room which you can't get into owing to the chaos of furniture, etc., alabaster statues, etc., piled up 4 or 5 feet high. Then we come to the sealed door behind which, I am sure, is the king and God knows what. Some of the stuff is in excellent condition, some is poor, but the whole thing is marvellous; and then there is that sealed door!! Even Lacau[1] was touched by the sight. [Two paragraphs omitted.] It is going to cost me something awful, but I am going to try to do it all myself. I think it will take Carter and three assistants nearly two years to remove, if we find much behind the seals. I am coming back in ten days and will try and see you.—Yours ever, CARNARVON."

Having found the archaeological "pearl of great price," with characteristic generosity he was anxious that all who could should come to Luxor to see it and to rejoice over it with him. He made an arrangement with The *Times* to publish detailed accounts of the clearing of the outer chambers, and to reproduce the splendid photographs of the most striking objects, which were made for him by a member of the American Archæological Mission, and thus people in all parts of the world were able to watch almost daily the progress of the work. Visitors from many countries thronged to Luxor to see Tutānkhāmen's tomb and the wonders that it contained, and Lord Carnarvon

[1] The present Director of the Service of Antiquities.

spent himself freely in helping them in every way in his power. He gave them his time and energy and knowledge ungrudgingly, but this work, alas! used up his strength and exhausted him. He was not physically a strong or robust man, and the effects of a serious motor accident, sustained many years ago, and of two illnesses in recent years, had taken toll of his vitality. His spirit and courage were invincible, nothing could daunt those, but the work that he had imposed upon himself was too exhausting for him. Then, when he was overtired and overworked, came the mosquito bite on his face. Every traveller in Egypt who has been the victim of the malignant and deadly mosquitoes, which are blown into the country in millions by the hot south winds in March and April, knows how serious are the fever and prostration that follow their successful attacks on the human body. The days passed and his work increased, and, as he refused to spare himself, serious illness came upon him, and he was obliged to go to Cairo and place himself in the hands of the doctors. There everything that medical science and skill could devise was done for him, but little by little he sank, and early in the morning of April 5 he passed peacefully away. The sympathy of the whole world went forth to him as he lay in that sick chamber in Cairo, fighting his fight with Death; that he should die so soon after winning such a glorious triumph seemed incredible.

The death of Lord Carnarvon is a serious blow for Egyptian Archæology, and his loss is irreparable.

For sixteen long years he devoted himself to excavations in Egypt, and he gave to them time, energy, and money on a scale which no other archaeologist has ever done. The spirit of Ancient Egypt gripped him nearly twenty years ago, and every year that passed strengthened its hold upon him. The dry bones of Egyptian philology left him cold, and when Egyptologists squabbled over dates and chronology in his presence his chuckle was a delightful thing to hear. But he was fired by the exquisite beauty of form and colour which he found in the antiquities of Egypt, and his collection of small Egyptian antiquities at Highclere Castle is, for its size, probably the most perfect known. He only cared for the best, and nothing but the best would satisfy him, and having obtained the best he persisted in believing that there must be somewhere something better than the best ! His quest for the beautiful in Egyptian design, form, and colour became the cult of his life in recent years. His taste was faultless, and his instinct for the true and genuine was unrivalled. When compared with a beautiful " antica " money had no value for him, and he was wont to say, with Sir Henry Rawlinson, " It is easier to get money than anticas." His work in Egypt brought him into contact with natives of all kinds, and he was universally popular with them, and he will be remembered for a long time as a generous employer and friend. His keen sense of humour, his quick wit, his capacity for understanding a matter swiftly, his ready sympathy, and his old-world courtesy appealed greatly to the governing classes in Egypt, and endeared him to his friends, who were legion, both Oriental and Occidental. Here I have only ventured to speak of Lord Carnarvon as the great and disinterested archaeologist, who gave years of his life and untold treasure for the sake of his love for science, for I have neither the knowledge nor the ability to deal with his successes as a pioneer of colour photography, and as a collector of prints, pictures, books, etc. These, and many of the phases of his character and pursuits, are treated felicitously and sympathetically in a careful appreciation of his life and character which appeared in The *Times*, published on the day of his burial on Beacon Hill (April 30).

E. A. WALLIS BUDGE.

British Museum,

May 7, 1923.

THE REIGN OF TUTĀNKHȦMEN.

 ("Living Image of Ȧmen"), King of Egypt, about B.C. 1400.

WHEN and where TUTĀNKHȦMEN was born is unknown, and there is some doubt about the identity of his father. From a scarab which was found in the temple of Osiris at Abydos,[1] we learn that his mother was called Merit-Rā  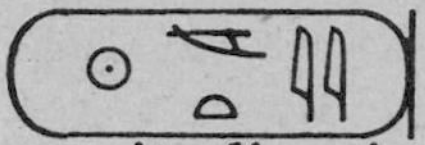. In the inscription on the red granite lion in the Southern Egyptian Gallery in the British Museum (No. 431), he says that he "restored the monuments of his father, King of the South and North, Lord of the Two Lands, Nebmaātrā, the emanation of Rā, the son of Rā, Ȧmenḥetep (III), Governor of Thebes." It is possible that Tutānkhȧmen was the son of Ȧmenḥetep III by one of his concubines, and that when he calls this king his father the statement is literally true, but there is no proof of it. On the other hand, Tutānkhȧmen may have used the word "father" simply as a synonym of "predecessor." The older Egyptologists accepted the statement made by him on the lion that he dedicated to the Temple of Sulb in Nubia as true, but some of the more recent writers reject it. The truth is that the name of Tutānkhȧmen's father is unknown. He became king of Egypt by

[1] See Mariette, *Abydos*, Paris, 1880, tom. II, pl. 40N.

virtue of his marriage with princess ȦNKHSEN-PAȦTEN, the third daughter of Ȧmenḥetep IV, 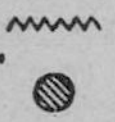 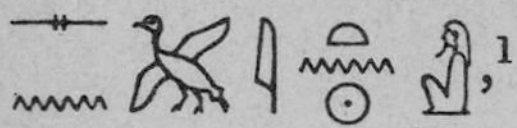,[1] at least that is what it is natural to suppose, but it is possible that he got rid of his immediate predecessor, Smenkhkarā, or Seāakarā, who married the princess MERITȦTEN, or ȦTENMERIT, 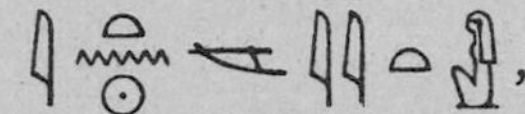, the eldest daughter of Ȧmenḥetep IV, and usurped his throne.

When Tutānkhȧmen ascended the throne he was, or at all events he professed to be, an adherent of the cult of Ȧten, or the "Solar Disk," and to hold the religious views of his wife and his father-in-law. Proof of this is provided by the fragment of a calcareous stone stele preserved at Berlin (No. 14197), on which he is described as "Lord of the Two Lands, Rākheperuneb, Lord of the Crowns, Tutānkhȧten , to whom life is given for ever."[2] He did not at once sever his connection with the cult of Ȧten, for he started work on a temple, or some other building, of Ȧten at Thebes. This is certain from the fact that several of the blocks of stone which Ḥeremḥeb, one of his immediate successors, used in his buildings bear Tutānkhȧmen's name. It is impossible to describe the extent of Tutānkhȧmen's building operations, for this same Ḥeremḥeb claimed much of his work as his own, and cut out wherever possible Tutānkhȧmen's name and inserted his own in its place. He went so far as to usurp the famous stele of Tutānkhȧmen

[1] This name means "Her life is of Ȧten" (*i.e.*, of the Solar Disk).

[2] See *Aegyptische Zeitschrift*, Bd. 38, 1900, pp. 112–114.

that Legrain discovered at Karnak in 1905.[1]
From this stele we learn that the " strong names "
and official titles which Tutānkhȧmen adopted
were as follows :—

1. Horus name. KA-NEKHT-TUT-MES

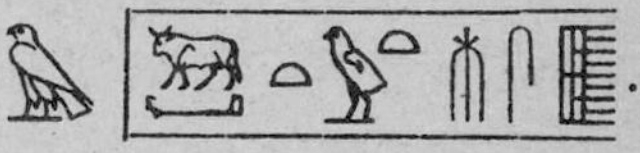

2. Nebti name. NEFER-HEPU-S-GERḤ TAUI.

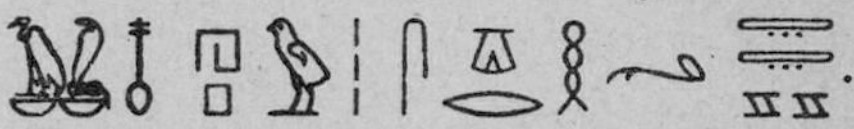

3. Golden Horus name. RENP-KHĀU-S-ḤETEP-

NETERU

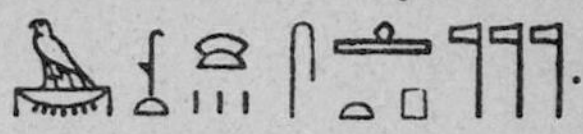

4. Nesu bȧt name. NEB-KHEPERU-RĀ

5. Son of Rā name. TUTĀNKHȦMEN

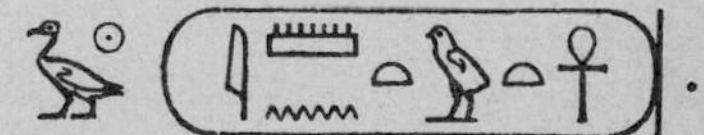

In some cases the cartouche of the nomen
contains the signs, which mean " governor
of Ȧnu of the South " (i.e., Hermonthis). When
Tutānkhȧten ascended the throne he changed
his name to Tutānkhȧmen, i.e., " Living image of
Ȧmen."
Our chief authority for the acts of Tutānkhȧmen
is the stele in Cairo already referred to, and from
the text, which unfortunately is mutilated in
several places, we can gain a very good idea of the

<hr />

[1] See *Annales du Service*, Vol. V, 1905, p. 192 ; *Recueil de
Travaux*, Vol. XXIX, 1907, pp. 162–173.

state of confusion that prevailed in Egypt when he ascended the throne. The hieroglyphs giving the year in which the stele was dated are broken away. The first lines give the names and titles of the king, who says that he was beloved of Åmen-Rā, the great god of Thebes, of Temu and Rā-Ḥeraakhuti, gods of Ånu (Heliopolis), Ptaḥ of Memphis, and Thoth, the Lord of the "words of god" (*i.e.*, hieroglyphs and the sacred writings). He calls himself the "good son of Åmen, born of Kamutef," and says that he sprang from a glorious seed and a holy egg, and that the god Åmen himself had begotten him. Åmen built his body, and fashioned him, and perfected his form, and the Divine Souls of Ånu were with him from his youth up, for they had decreed that he was to be an eternal king, and an established Horus, who would devote all his care and energies to the service of the gods who were his fathers.

These statements are of great interest, for when understood as the king meant them to be understood, they show that his accession to the throne of Egypt was approved of by the priesthoods of Heliopolis, Memphis, Hermopolis and Thebes. Whatever sympathy he may have possessed for the Cult of Åten during the lifetime of Åmenhetep IV had entirely disappeared when he set up his great stele at Karnak, and it is quite clear that he was then doing his utmost to fulfil the expectations of the great ancient priesthoods of Egypt.

The text continues: He made to flourish again the monuments which had existed for centuries, but which had fallen into ruin [during the reign of Åakhunåten]. He put an end to rebellion and disaffection 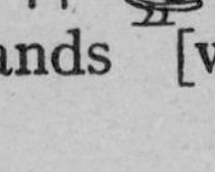. Truth marched through the Two Lands [which he established firmly]. When His Majesty became King of the South the whole country was in a state of chaos, similar to that in which it had been in primeval times (*i.e.*, at the Creation). From Abu (Elephantine) to the Swamps [of the Delta] the properties of the temples of the gods and goddesses had been [destroyed], their shrines were in a state of ruin and their estates had become a desert. Weeds grew in the courts of the temples. The sanctuaries were overthrown and the sacred sites had become thoroughfares for the people. The land had perished, the gods were sick unto death, and the country was set behind their backs.

The state of general ruin throughout the country was, of course, largely due to the fact that the treasuries of the great gods received no income or tribute on any great scale from the vassal tribes of Palestine and Syria. It is easy to understand that the temple buildings would fall into ruin, and the fields go out of cultivation when once the power of the central authority was broken. Tutānkhāmen next says that if an envoy were sent to Tchah 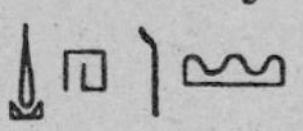 (Syria) to broaden the frontiers of Egypt, 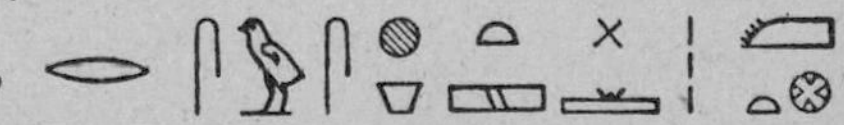, his mission did not prosper; in other words, the collectors of tribute returned empty-handed because the tribes would not pay it. And it was useless to appeal to any god or any goddess, for there was no reply made to the entreaties of petitioners. The hearts of the gods were disgusted with the people, and they destroyed the creatures that they had made. But the days wherein such things were passed by, and at length His Majesty ascended the throne of his father, and began to regulate and govern the lands of Horus, *i.e.*, the temple-towns and their estates. Egypt and the Red Land (*i.e.*, Desert) came under his supervision, and every land greeted his will with bowings of submission.

The text goes on to say that His Majesty was living in the Great House which was in Per-Āakheperkarā. This palace was probably situated either in a suburb of Memphis or in some district at no great distance from that city. (Some think that it was in or quite near Thebes.) Here "he reigned like Rā in heaven," and he devoted himself to the carrying out of the "plan of this land." He pondered deeply in his mind on his courses of action, and communed with his own heart how to do the things that would be acceptable to the people. It was to be expected that, when once he had discarded Åten and all his works, he would have gone and taken up his abode in Thebes, and entered into direct negotiations with the priests of Åmen. In other words, Tutānkhåmen was not certain as to the kind of reception he would meet with at Thebes, and therefore he went northwards, and lived in or near Memphis. Whilst here "he sought after the welfare of father Åmen," and he cast a figure of his "august emanation," 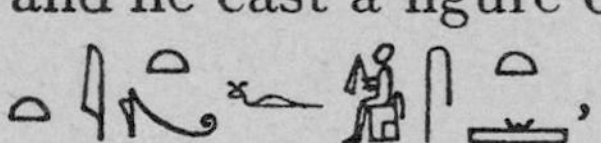, in gold, or silver-gold. Moreover, he did more than had ever been done before to enhance the power and splendour of Åmen. The text unfortunately gives no description of the figure of Åmen which he made in gold, but a very good idea of what it was like may be gained from the magnificent solid gold figure of the god that is in the Carnarvon Collection at Highclere Castle, and was exhibited at the Burlington Fine Arts Club in 1922. A handsome silver figure of Åmen-Rā, plated with gold, is exhibited in the British Museum (Fifth Egyptian

Room, Table-case I, No. 42). This must have come from a shrine of the god. He next fashioned a figure of "Father Āmen" on thirteen staves, a portion of which was decorated with gold *tchām* (*i.e.*, gold or silver-gold), lapis lazuli and all kinds of valuable stones; formerly the figure of Āmen only possessed eleven (?) staves. He also made a figure of Ptaḥ, south of his wall, the Lord of Life, and a portion of this likewise was decorated with gold or silver-gold, lapis lazuli, turquoises and all kinds of valuable gems. The figure of Ptaḥ, which originally stood in the shrine in Memphis, only possessed six (?) staves. Besides this, Tutānkhāmen built monuments to all the gods, and he made the sacred images, , of them of real *tchām* metal, which was the best produced. He built their sanctuaries anew, taking care to have durable work devoted to their construction; he established a system of divine offerings, and made arrangements for the maintenance of the same. His endowments provided for a daily supply of offerings to all the temples, and on a far more generous scale than was originally contemplated.

He introduced () or appointed libationers and ministrants of the gods, whom he chose from among the sons of the principal men in their villages, who were known to be of good reputation, and provided for their increased stipends by making gifts to their temples of immense quantities of gold, silver, bronze and other metals. He filled the temples with servants, male and female, and with gifts which had formed part of the booty captured by him. In addition to the presents which he gave to the priests and servants of the temples, he increased the revenues of the temples, some twofold, some threefold and others fourfold, by means of additional gifts of *tchām* metal, gold, lapis lazuli, turquoises, precious stones of all kinds, royal cloth of byssus, flax-linen, oil, unguents, perfumes, incense, *ȧhmit* 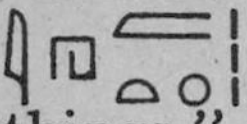 and myrrh. Gifts of " all beautiful things " were given lavishly by the king. Having re-endowed the temples, and made provision for the daily offerings and for the performance of services which were performed every day for the benefit of the king, that is to say, himself, Tutānkhȧmen made provision for the festal processions on the river and on the sacred lakes of the temples. He collected men who were skilful in boat-building, and made them to build boats of new acacia wood of the very best quality that could be obtained in the country of Negau . Many parts of the boats were plated with gold, and their effulgence lighted up the river.

The information contained in the last two paragraphs enables us to understand the extent of the ruin that had fallen upon the old religious institutions of the country through the acts of Ȧakhunȧten. The temple walls were mutilated by the Ȧtenites, the priesthoods were driven out, and all temple properties were confiscated and applied to the propagation of the cult of Ȧten. The figures of the great gods that were made of gold and other precious metals in the shrines were melted down, and thus the people could not consult their gods in their need, for the gods had no figures wherein to dwell, even if they wished to come upon the earth. There were no priests left in the land, no gods to entreat, no funeral ceremonies could be performed, and the dead had to be laid in their tombs without the blessing of the priests.

During this period of religious chaos, which obtained throughout the country, a number of slaves, both male and female, and singing men, , *shemāiu*, and men of the acrobat class, , had been employed by the Åtenite king to assist in the performance of his religious services, and at festivals celebrated in honour of Åten. These Tutānkhåmen "purified" and transferred to the royal palace, where they performed the duties of servants of some kind in connection with the services of all the "father-gods." This treatment by the king was regarded by them as an act of grace, and they were exceedingly content with their new positions. The concluding lines of the stele tell us little more than that the gods and goddesses of Egypt rejoiced once more in beholding the performance of their services, that the old order of worship was re-established, and that all the people of Egypt thanked the king for his beneficent acts from the bottom of their hearts. The gods gave the king life and serenity, and by the help of Rā, Ptaḥ and Thoth he administered his country with wisdom, and gave righteous judgments daily to all the people.

In line 18 on the Stele of Tutānkhåmen it is stated that the gifts made by the king to the priests and temples were part of the booty which His Majesty had captured from conquered peoples . This suggests that even during his short reign of from eight to ten years he managed to make raids—they cannot be called wars—in the countries which his predecessors had conquered and made dependencies of Egypt. The truth of his statement is fully proved by the pictures and inscriptions found in the tomb of Ḥui 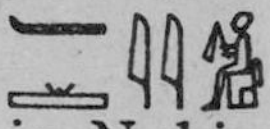 in Western Thebes. This officer served in Nubia under Åmenḥetep IV, and as a reward for his fidelity and success the king made him Prince of Kesh (Nubia), and gave him full authority to rule from Nekhen, the modern Al-kâb, about 50 miles south of Thebes, to Nest-Taui 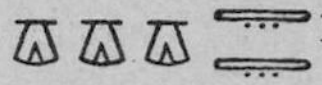[1] or Napata (Jabal Barkal), at the foot of the Fourth Cataract. During the reign of Tutānkhåmen Ḥui returned from Nubia to Thebes, bringing with him large quantities of gold, both in the form of rings and dust, vessels of gold and silver, bags full of precious stones, Sûdânî beds, couches, chairs of state, shields and a chariot.[2] With these precious objects came the shêkh of Måām, the shêkh of Uait, the sons of all the principal chiefs on both sides of the river from Buhen (Wâdî Ḥalfah) to Elephantine, and a considerable number of slaves. Ḥui and his party arrived in six boats, and when all the gifts were unloaded they were handed over to Tutānkhåmen's officials, who had gone to receive them. It is not easy to decide whether this presentation of the produce of Nubia by Ḥui was an official delivery of tribute due to Tutānkhåmen, or a personal offering to the new king of Egypt. If Ḥui was appointed Viceroy of Kesh by Åmenḥetep IV or his father, it is possible that he was an adherent of the cult of Åten. In this case, his gifts to Tutānkhåmen were probably personal, and were offered to him by Ḥui with the set

[1] This is a name of Thebes, but it was also applied to the town of Napata, where the great temple of Åmen-Rā of Nubia was situated.

[2] See the drawing published by Lepsius, *Denkmäler* III, pl. 116–118.

Plate I.

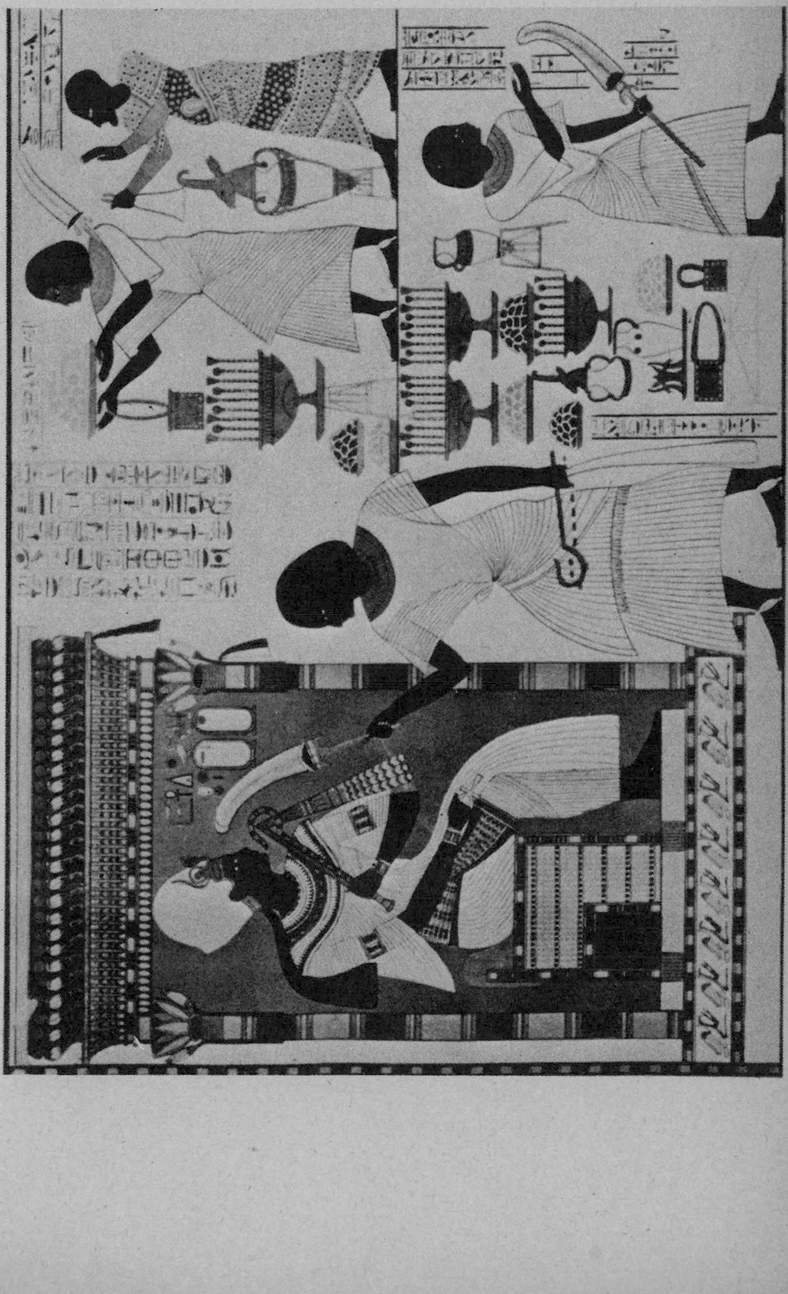

Ḥui presenting tribute and gifts from vassal peoples to Tutānkhamen. From Lepsius, *Denkmäler* III, 117.

Red granite lion with an inscription on the base stating that it was made by Tutānkhāmen. It was dedicated by him to the Temple of Sulb, in the Third Cataract in the Egyptian Sûdân, when he "restored the monuments of his father, 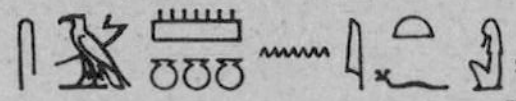, Åmenḥetep III."

British Museum, Southern Egyptian Gallery, No. 431.

purpose of placating the restorer of the cult of Âmen. Be this as it may, the gold and silver and precious stones from Nubia were most acceptable to the king, for they supplied him with means for the re-endowment of the priests and the temples.

Egyptologists, generally, have agreed that the scenes in Ḥui's tomb representing the presentation of gifts from Nubia have a historical character, and that we may consider that Tutānkhâmen really exercised rule in Nubia. But there are also painted on the walls scenes in which the chiefs and nobles of Upper Retennu  (Syria) are presenting the same kinds of gifts to Tutānkhâmen, and these cannot be so easily accepted as being historical in character. In his great inscription, Tutānkhâmen says explicitly that during the reign of Âakhunâten it was useless to send missions to Syria to "enlarge the frontiers of Egypt," for they never succeeded in doing so. But he does not say that he himself did not send missions, *i.e.*, make raids, into some parts of Phoenicia and Syria, and it is possible that he did. It is also possible that some of the Syrian chiefs, hearing of the accession of a king who was following the example of Thothmes III and honouring Âmen, sent gifts to him with the view of obtaining the support of Egyptian arms against their foes.

Exactly when and how Tutānkhâmen died is not known, and his age at the time of his death cannot be stated. No tomb of his has been found in the mountains of Tall al-'Amârnah, and, up to the present, there is no evidence that he had a tomb specially hewn for him in the Valley of the Tombs of the Kings. During the course of his excavations in this Valley, Mr. Theodore Davis found a tomb which he believed to be that of

Tutānkhâmen.[1] In it there was a broken box containing several pieces of gold leaf stamped with the names of Tutānkhâmen and his wife Ānkhsenâmen, etc. In a pit some distance from this tomb he discovered what he took to be the débris from a tomb, such as dried wreaths of leaves and flowers. The cover of a very large jar, which had been broken, was wrapped up in a cloth on which was inscribed the name of Tutānkhâmen. One of the most beautiful objects found by Davis was the little blue glazed funerary vase which is figured on plate XCII of his book. It was discovered in a sort of hiding place under a large rock, and bears the inscription "Beautiful god, Neb-kheperu Rā, giver of life"  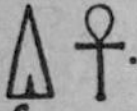. These facts certainly suggest that Davis found *a* tomb of Tutānkhâmen.

The objects in the British Museum that bear the name of Tutānkhâmen are few, the largest and most important being the granite lion which he placed in the temple built by Âmenhetep III at Sulb (the "Soleb" of Lepsius), about half-way up the Third Cataract on the left or west bank. Several scarabs[2] and a bead bearing his prenomen or nomen are exhibited in Table-Case B. (Fourth Egyptian Room), and also the fragment of a model of a boomerang in blue glazed faïence in Wall-Case 225 (Fifth Egyptian Room), No. 54822. Two fine porcelain tubes for stibium, or eye-paint, are exhibited in Wall-Case 272 (Sixth Egyptian Room). The one (No. 27376) has a dark bluish green colour and is inscribed "Beautiful god, Lord of the Two Lands, Lord of Crowns, Neb-

[1] See Davis-Maspero-Daressy, *The Tombs of Harmhabi and Touat-ânkhamanou*, London, 1912.

[2] See Hall, H. R., *Catalogue of Egyptian Scarabs*, London, 1913, Nos. 1968–1972, pp. 197, 198.

kheperu-Rā, giver of life for ever" 
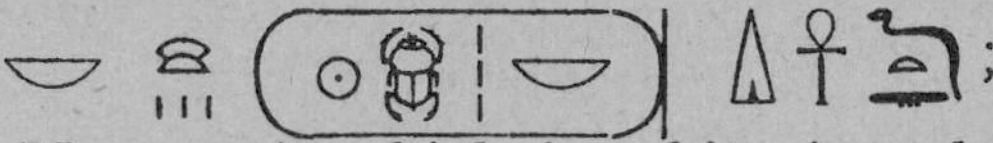; and the other (No. 2573), which is white in colour, is inscribed with the names of his wife and himself :— 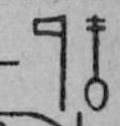
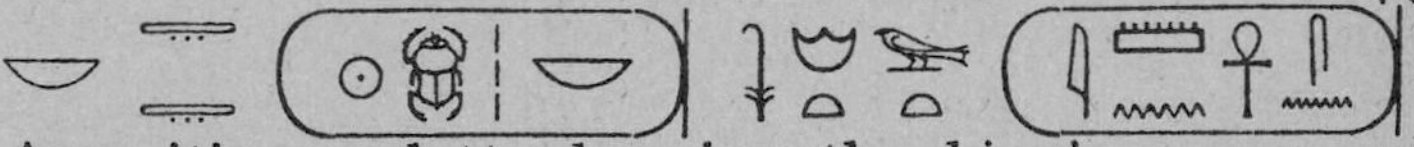.
A writing palette bearing the king's prenomen[1] was found at Ḳurnah during the time of the French Expedition, and this and the other objects mentioned above suggest that the royal tomb was being plundered during the early years of the XIXth century.

An interesting mention is made of Tutānkh-âmen in one of the tablets from Boghaz Keui, and it suggests that communications passed more or less frequently between the kings of the Hittites at that period and the kings of Egypt. The document is written in cuneiform characters[2] in the Hittite language, and states that the Queen of Egypt, called Da-kha-mu-un  wrote to the father of the reigning Hittite king to tell him that her husband Bi-ib-khu-ru-ri-ya-ash  was dead, and that she had no son, and that she wanted one, and she asked him to send to her one of his many sons, and him she would make her husband.[3] Now Bibkhururiyaash is nothing more nor less than a transcription of NEB-KHEPERU-RĀ, the prenomen of king Tutānkhâmen.

[1]  This is the legend as printed in Champollion, *Monuments*, tom. II, pl. CXCI *bis* No. 2.

[2] For the text see *Keilschrift aus Boghazköi*, Heft V, No. 6. Rev. III, ll. 7–13.

[3] See Dr. F. Hrosny, *Die Lösung des Hethitischen Problems*, in the *Mitteilungen der Deutschen Orient-Gesellschaft*, December, 1915, No. 56, p. 36.

TUTĀNKHÅMEN AND THE CULT OF ÅMEN.

THE early history of the god Åmen is somewhat obscure, and his origin is unknown. The name Åmen [hieroglyphs] means "hidden (one)," a title which might be applied to many gods. A god

Åmen-Rā, King of the Gods, Great Lord of Thebes.

The goddess Åmenit, a female counterpart of Åmen, dweller in the Northern Apt (Karnak).

Åmen and his consort Åment or Åmenit are mentioned in the Pyramid Texts (UNÅS, line 558), where they are grouped with Nåu and Nen, and with the two Lion gods Shu and Tefnut. This Åmen was regarded as an ancient nature-god by the priests of Heliopolis under the Vth dynasty, and it is possible that many of his attributes were transferred at a very early period to Åmen, the great god of Thebes. Though recent excavations have shown that a cult of Åmen existed at Thebes under the Ancient Empire, it is doubtful if it possessed any more than a local importance until the XIIth dynasty. When the princes of Thebes conquered their rivals in the north and obtained the sovereignty of Egypt, their god Åmen and his priesthood became a great power in the land, and an entirely new temple was built by them, in his honour, at Karnak on the right bank of the Nile. The temple was quite small, and resembled in form and arrangement some of the small Nubian temples; it consisted of a shrine, with a few small chambers grouped about it, and a forecourt, with a colonnade on two sides of it. Åmen was not the oldest god worshipped there, and his sanctuary seems to have absorbed the shrine of the ancient goddess Åpit. The name of Thebes is derived from T-Åpe, the Coptic name of the shrine of the goddess Åpit, and the city was not known as Nut Åmen 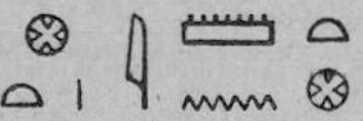 (the No Amon of the Bible, Nahum 3, 8), *i.e.*, the "city of Åmen," until a very much later date.

Although the kings of the XIIth dynasty were Thebans it is possible that they and many of their finest warriors had Sûdânî blood in their veins, and the attributes that they ascribed to Åmen were similar to those that the Nubian peoples assigned to their indigenous gods. To them Åmen symbolized the hidden but irresistible power that produces conception and growth in human beings and in the animal and vegetable worlds. And in some places in Egypt, and Nubia and the Oases, the symbol of the god Åmen was either the umbilicus[1] or the gravid womb. The symbol of Åmen that was shown to Alexander the Great, when he visited the temple of Jupiter Ammon in the Oasis of Sîwâh, was an object closely resembling the umbilicus, and it was inlaid with emeralds (turquoises ?) and other precious stones—umbilico maxime similis est habitus, smaragdo et gemmis coagmentatus.[2] The name of Åmen was carried into Nubia and the Egyptian Sûdân by the kings of the XIIth dynasty when they made raids into those countries, and his worship took root there readily and flourished. The booty which was brought back to Thebes was shared by them with Åmen, and many captives and slaves were set apart as the property of the god. Soon Åmen gained the reputation of the god of successful warriors, and his fame grew and spread abroad, and little by little the attributes and powers of the older gods of Heliopolis, Memphis and Abydos were united to his own in the minds of his priests and followers.

Under the rule of the kings of the XVIIIth dynasty the glory and power of Åmen waxed greater and greater, and his fame spread through the Eastern Desert and Syria. As he gave victory to the kings of the XIIth dynasty in Nubia, so he now gave undreamed of success to Egyptian arms in Western Asia ; and the Pharaohs returned to Thebes laden with spoil of every kind and with rich gifts from the non-combatant peoples in

[1] See Daressy, *Une Nouvelle Forme d'Amon* in *Annales du Service des Antiquités de l'Egypte*, tome IX, p. 64 ff.

[2] Quintus Curtius, lib. IV, §7. See also Naville, *Le Dieu de l'Oasis de Jupiter-Amon* in *Comptes Rendus de l'Académie*, 1906, p. 25.

Phœnicia and Syria. And Åmen might well be declared to be the "god of the world," especially during the reign of Thothmes III. Never before had such wealth flowed into the treasury of the temple of Åmen, or Åmen-Rā, as he began to be called, and never before had the power of his priests been so great. Åmenḥetep I, the second king of the dynasty, had been a strong supporter of the cult of Åmen, and he seems to have been the founder of the order of the priests of Åmen, and certainly endowed the temple in the Northern Åpt with great wealth. His prenomen and nomen are often seen occupying prominent places on the coffins of the priests of Åmen. The work of establishing the order begun by Åmenḥetep I was consolidated and extended by Thothmes III, who set the priesthood in order, appointed a high priest, and provided them with rich revenues and gave them large estates for their maintenance. The gifts that the temple of Åmen received as a result of the seventeen expeditions made by Thothmes III into Phoenicia and Syria, and into the country in the neighbourhood of the waters of the Upper Euphrates, and the share of the tribute received from Cyprus and the Sûdân must have been well-nigh incalculable. The treasury of Åmen was so well supplied by Thothmes III, and the affairs of his priesthood so well regulated by him, that his two immediate successors, Åmenḥetep II and Thothmes IV, were not called upon to make extraordinary raids into Western Asia for the purpose of collecting spoil.

Åmenḥetep II, about B.C. 1500, devoted his energies to the conquest of the southern portion of the Egyptian Sûdân, which he penetrated as far as Wâd Bâ-Nagaa, a district lying about 80 miles to the north of the modern city of Khartûm. But it is doubtful if he possessed any

effective hold on the Sûdân beyond Napata
(Jabal Barkal), at the foot of the Fourth
Cataract. During one of his wars, or raids, into
Syria, he slew a rebel chief and sent his body to
Napata to be hung upon the city walls, so that
the natives might see it and tremble. We may
be sure that the priesthood of Ȧmen at Thebes
took great care to inform their colleagues at
Napata that it was their god Ȧmen who had given
the king the victory. Ȧmenḥetep II was a loyal
servant of Ȧmen, for on the stele which he set up
after his return from Upper Rethennu he says that
he came back " with a heart expanded with joy
to Father Ȧmen because he had overthrown all
his enemies, and enlarged the frontiers of Egypt,
and had slain seven chiefs with his own club whilst
they were living in Thekhsi, and had hung their
bodies up head downwards on the bows of his
boat as he sailed up the Nile to Thebes."

Ȧmenḥetep II was succeeded about B.C. 1450 by
his son Thothmes IV, who seems to have owed his
accession to the throne, not to the priests of Ȧmen,
but to the priests of Heliopolis. His mother was
not of royal rank, and it is probable that her
religious sympathies were with the old solar gods
of Heliopolis rather than with Ȧmen, or Ȧmen-Rā,
of Thebes. On a huge red granite stele, which
stands between the paws of the Sphinx at Gîzah
immediately in front of its breast, is cut an important inscription which throws light on the subject
of the accession to the throne of Thothmes IV.
According to the text, the young prince Thothmes
was hunting at Gîzah and sat down to rest himself
under the shadow of the Sphinx. Whilst there he
fell asleep, and thef ourfold Sun-god, Ḥerȧakhuti-
Kheperȧ-Rā-Tem, appeared to him in a dream
and promised him the crowns of Egypt if he would
clear away from the Sphinx and his temple the

desert sand, which had swallowed them up. Now the Sphinx was believed to be the image and dwelling-place of Temu-Ḥerȧakhuti, a solar god in whom were united the attributes and powers of Tem, the oldest sun-god of Heliopolis, and Ḥerȧakhuti, a still older sun-god. Thothmes did as the god wished, that is to say, as the priests of Heliopolis wished, and by so doing forwarded their

Ḥerȧakhuti, *i.e.*, Horus of the Two Horizons, the Great God. Rā, the mid-day form of the Sun-god, is often depicted in this form.

Temu, Lord of the Two Lands, of Ȧnu (On) Great God, Governor of the Nine Gods. He was probably the oldest man-headed god in Egypt.

political aspirations and secured their assistance in obtaining the throne. During his short reign of about nine years Thothmes IV made raids into Syria and the Egyptian Sûdân, and the temple of Ȧmen no doubt obtained a share in the spoil which he brought back—in fact, an inscription at Karnak contains a list of the gifts that he made to Āmen on his return from a very successful raid. We may note in passing that although the name of Āmen forms part of his personal name, his Nebti name was "Stablished in sovereignty like Tem."

The opening up of Western Asia by the victorious arms of Amasis I and his successors was followed by a great increase in the communications that passed between Egypt and the peoples of Syria, Mitanni, Assyria and Babylonia. The trade between these countries increased, and the merchant caravans carried not only the wares and products of one country into the other, but also information about the manners and customs and religions of the various peoples with whom they came in contact. Thothmes IV appears to have been the first Egyptian king who entered into friendly relations with the kings of Karaduniyash (Babylonia) and Mitanni. Tushratta, king of Mitanni, tells us, in a letter[1] which he sent to Āmenḥetep IV, that the father of his father, Āmenḥetep III, sent to his grandfather, Artatama, and asked for his daughter to wife; in other words, Thothmes IV wanted to marry a princess of Mitanni. Six times did Thothmes IV make his request in vain, and it was only after the seventh asking that the king of Mitanni gave his daughter to the king of Egypt. As Queen of Egypt she was styled "Hereditary Princess, Great Lady, President of the South and the North, Great Royal Mother, MUT-EM-UĀA."

.

The princess would naturally come to Egypt escorted by a number of her people, and it is very probable that she and her followers introduced into

[1] Preserved in Berlin; see Winckler, *Die Thontafeln von Tell-el-Amarna*, No. 24, p. 51.

Egypt religious views that were more in harmony with those of the priests of Heliopolis than of the votaries of Āmen.

Little is known of the kingdom of Mitanni and its people. There is one letter in Berlin written in the language of Mitanni, and the Assyriologists who have made a special study of it assign to the language a place among the "Caspian group," and are inclined to compare it with Georgian; and they give it an Aryan origin.[1] The names of four of their gods are mentioned in the text of a Treaty found at Boghaz Keui, and the Mitannians swore by them to observe this Treaty.[2] These gods are:—

Omitting the determinatives,[3] these names may be transliterated thus:— 1, Mi-it-ra-ash-shi-il. 2, U-ru-wa-na-ash-shi-il. 3, In-tar. 4, Na-sha-at-ti-ya-an-na. And their identifications with the Indian gods Mîtra (Mithras), Varuna, Indra and Nasatiya seem to be certain. The solar and celestial character of these Indian gods has much in common with that of the solar gods of Heliopolis, and if the princess of Mitanni who married Thothmes IV carried her worship of them into Egypt, it is easy to believe that her religious sympathy and support would be given to Tem and his cognate gods, and not to Āmen. With her arrival at Thebes there came an influence

[1] Bork, *Die Mitanni Sprache*, Berlin, 1909.

[2] *Keilschrifttexte aus Boghazköi.* Heft I, p. 7. No. 1, l. 55.

[3]  and  are determinatives of "god" and "gods."

which was hostile to Ȧmen, but her husband's reign was too short for it to produce any great material effect.

Thothmes IV was succeeded by his son by Queen Mutemuȧa, who ascended the throne under the name of Ȧmenḥetep (III); thus the name of the god Ȧmen once again formed part of the personal name of the reigning king. The meaning of this name, "Ȧmen is content, or satisfied," is significant. He reigned for about thirty-six years, probably in the latter half of the fifteenth century B.C. A legend[1] was current in Egypt under the Ancient Empire in which it was asserted that the god Rā came to earth and, assuming the form of a priest of Rā, the husband of one Ruṭṭeṭ, appeared to his wife and, companying with her, begot three sons, each of whom became King of all Egypt. From that time every king prefixed to his personal name the title SA RĀ,  "son of Rā." Nearly two thousand years later the great Queen Ḥatshepsut decorated her temple at Dêr al-Baḥarî with bas-reliefs, on which were sculptured scenes connected with her conception and birth. In these the god Ȧmen, in the human form of her father Thothmes I, is seen companying with Queen Ȧāhmes, and the inscriptions prove that Ḥatshepsut believed that she was of the god's seed and that his divine blood flowed in her veins.[2] As Ȧmen had in the XVIIIth dynasty assumed all the powers and attributes of Rā of Heliopolis, the father of the kings who ruled from Memphis, it was only fitting that he should assume human form and become the physical father of the kings who ruled from his city of Thebes. The same

1 See Erman, *Die Märchen des Papyrus Westcar*, Berlin, 1890.

2 See Naville's edition of the texts, Vol. II, pl. 46–55.

BAS-RELIEF REPRESENTING ÅMENḤETEP III AS AN INCARNATION OF ÅMEN-RĀ.

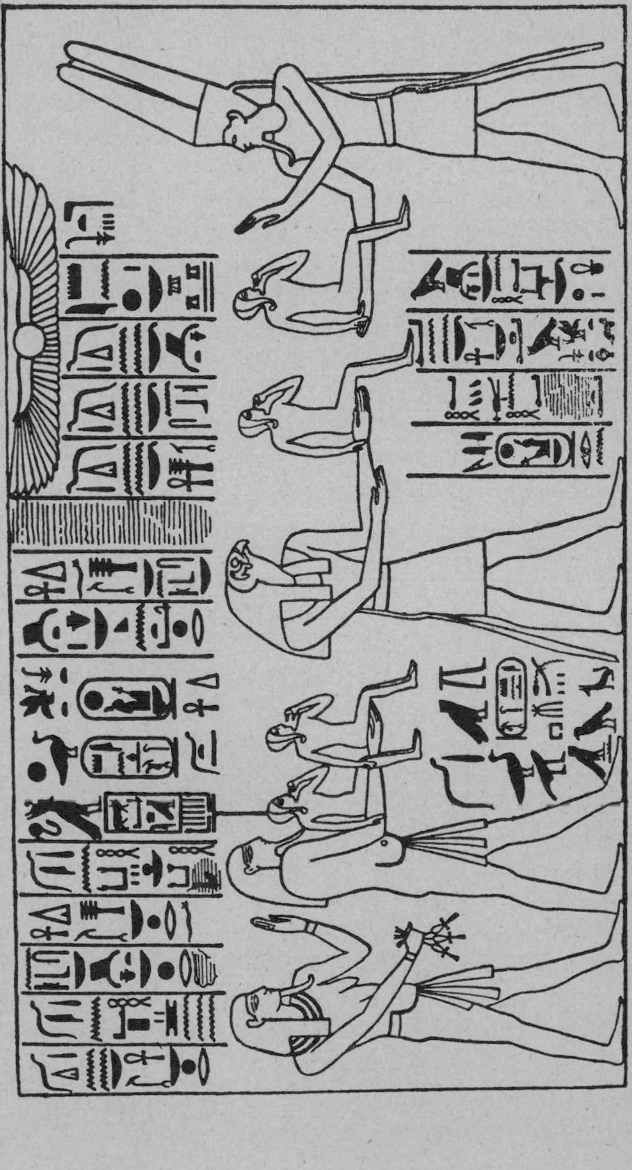

The Nile-god bringing offerings.

Heka holding Åmenhetep III and his Ka. Above the child are his names and titles, and above his Ka is his Horus name.

Horus presenting the divine child and his Ka to Åmen-Rā; Åmen-Rā acknowledging the child to be his son, and addressing him.

fiction was promulgated by the priests of Åmen in respect of their god and Åmenḥetep III. According to the bas-relief in the sanctuary of the temple which he built in the Northern Apt in honour of Åmen, Mut and Khensu, Åmen came to Queen Mutemuåa in the human form of Thothmes IV, and begot by her the son who reigned as Åmenḥetep III. Both scenes and texts were copied from the bas-reliefs in Ḥatshepsut's temple, which in turn were probably copied from some popular document compiled by the priests of Åmen at the beginning of the XVIIIth dynasty, perhaps with special reference to Åmenḥetep I.

Whatever views Åmenḥetep III held concerning Åmen and his worship, he did not allow them to interfere with or obstruct his public allegiance to that god. This fact is proved by his building operations at Luxor and the gifts which he made to the temples and priesthood of Åmen throughout the country. But he honoured other Egyptian gods besides Åmen, for he built a temple at Elephantine to Khnemu, a very ancient god of the region of the First Cataract. To commemorate his victory over the Nubians in the fifth year of his reign, he built the great temple called Ḥet Khā-em-Maāt 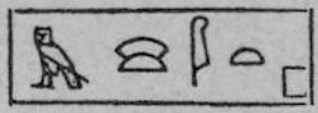 at Sulb, in the Egyptian Sûdân. He dedicated it to Father Åmen, Lord of the Thrones of the Two Lands, to Khnemu and to "his own Image living upon earth, Neb-maāt-Rā.[1]" On a bas-relief published by Lepsius[2] we see him worshipping himself, as Lord of Ta-Kenset. In several of the scenes sculptured on the walls he is represented making offerings to Åmen-Rā, Khnemu and other gods, and he is

[1] Neb-maāt-Rā is the prenomen of Åmenḥetep III.

[2] *Denkmäler*, III, 85.

Khnem, who became incarnate in a species of ram.

Ānqit, the female counterpart of Khnem.

Sati, daughter of Khnem and Ānqit.

The Triad of the First Cataract, in whose honour Åmenḥetep III built a temple at Elephantine.

frequently accompanied by his wife Ti. At Saddênga he built a temple to Ti as the goddess of the Sûdân.

In Egypt, at all events, the people were not prohibited from worshipping the old gods of

Ȧmenḥetep III worshipping himself as a member of the Triad in the Temple of Ṣulb.

the country, and that his own high officials did so openly is evident from the grey granite stele of the architects Ḥer and Suti in the British Museum.[1] The stele is in the form of the door of a tomb and has a plain cornice and a raised

[1] No. 475, Bay 9. Old No. 826. See *A Guide to the Egyptian Galleries*, p. 134.

border. In the upper part of the central panel are the two *utchats*, or eyes of the Sun and Moon , and the winged disk, and below these are figures of Osiris and Anubis; the figures of the architects and their wives are obliterated. In the inscriptions above the panel Ḥer beseeches: 1, Hathor of Thebes, the mistress of the goddesses,

Hathor of Thebes, who was incarnate in the forms of a cow and a woman.

Mut, Lady of Âsher, a female counterpart of Âmen-Rā.

to grant to him a coming forth into the presence [of the god]; 2, Khensu to give him all good, sweet and pleasant things; and 3, Hathor of Thebes to receive them in the temples. Suti beseeches: 1, Âmen-Rā to give him sepulchral meals in Hermonthis; 2, Mut to give him all good things; and 3, Hathor of the cemetery to give him beautiful life and pleasure upon earth.

On the right-hand side of the panel Ḥer beseeches: 1, Rā-Ḥeråakhuti, lord of heaven, to let him see Åten and to look at the Moon as he did upon earth; 2, Ånpu (Anubis) to give him a beautiful funeral after old age and a burial in the western part of Thebes; and 3, the divine Queen Nefertåri to give him the sweet breath of the north wind, coolness and wine, and a coming forth into the presence [of the God].

On the left-hand side of the panel Suti beseeches: 1, Osiris, Governor of eternity, to give him cakes and offerings in the presence of Un-Nefer; 2, Seker, lord of the coffin chamber, to let him go in and out of the underworld, without obstruction to his soul, at pleasure; and 3, Isis, the mother of the god, to grant him power to move freely about in the Peqa (at Abydos) under a decree of the great god.

Here, then, we have these two high officials, the one overseer of the works in the temple of Karnak, and the other overseer of the works in the temple of Luxor, men of learning and culture, praying for the goodwill, help and favour of Hathor of the city, of Hathor of the cemetery, of Mut, the consort of Åmen, of Khensu, son of Åmen and Mut, of the old Sun-god Rā-Ḥeråakhuti, of Ånpu, god of the tomb, of Nefertåri, the deified Queen of Amasis I, of Osiris, god and judge of the dead, of Isis, his consort, and of Seker, the old god of the Underworld of Memphis. Åmen is not mentioned with these old gods, into whose hands Ḥer and Suti were content to commit their souls after death. But Åmen was the great god of their city, and to him they owed their occupation and daily bread, and they acknowledged his power in the hymn which they caused to be cut on the panel of their funerary stele. The importance of this hymn is considerable, for the stele is dated, in line 15, by the mention of the name of the king they served, Åmenḥetep III. It is quite short, consisting of less than eight lines, and it tells us little about Åmen. The opening words say that it is a hymn to Åmen when he rises as Ḥeràakhuti; that is to say, it is addressed to Åmen in his character of a solar god. It might equally well be addressed

Khensu, a Moon-god, third member of the great Theban Triad Åmen-Rā, Mut and Khensu.

Ånpu, or Anubis, son of Set and Nephthys.

to Rā or Horus or any solar god. The writer calls the god a "daily beauty that never fails to rise," and identifies him with Kheperà, an ancient god of creation, who is mighty in works. His rays which strike the face cannot be known (or estimated), and the brilliantly bright and shining metal called *tchām* cannot be compared for splendour with his beautiful appearance. The caps on the pyramidions of obelisks were made of *tchām* metal, and the brightness of them could be seen many leagues away. In line 3 Åmen is said to have been *ptaḥ-tu*, *i.e.*, he was "designed," just as an object is designed, or plotted out, by a draughtsman, and the correct meaning of the

Sebåk, an ancient Crocodile-god.

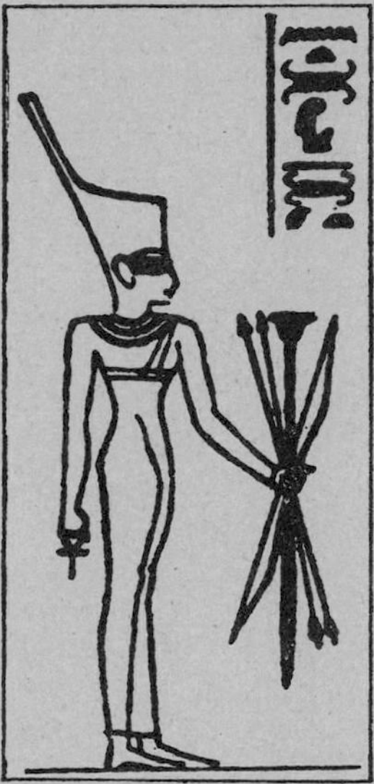

Net (Neith), the female counterpart of Sebåk, or Sebek.

word may be that Åmen designed his own form. Next the god "plated his limbs," *i.e.*, he made them to have the appearance of plates made of *tchām* metal. This statement is followed by the words, "[He] gives birth, but was not himself born: Only One in his characteristics, qualities, powers and operations."

Thus we learn that Åmen was, like Kheperå, self-designed, self-created, self-existent in a form that was never born as ordinary creatures are, and that he was One and Alone without equal, or fellow, or counterpart. The writer next refers to the duration of the god's existence, as the traverser of eternity, and the passer over the roads of millions of years with his form. His splendour is the splendour of heaven, and though "all men see his passage, he is

Ḥer-Semsu, or Horus the Aged.

Ḥer-pa-khart (Harpokrates), or Horus the Child.

hidden from their faces" (in his character of the "hidden" god). He travels over the celestial waters vast distances in a moment of time every day. There is no cessation in his work, and every one sees him, never ceasing to do so. When he sets he rises upon the denizens of the Ṭuat, and his rays force their way into the eyes [of the dead] (?) When he sets in the western horizon men fall asleep and become motionless like the dead. With these words the Hymn to Åmen comes to an end.

But during the lifetime of these twin brothers, Ḥer and Suti, the cult of Åten must have made considerable progress at Thebes, for, in spite of their loyalty to Åmen, and to the old solar gods of the country, and to Osiris and Isis being manifest, they caused a Hymn to Åten to be engraved on their funerary stele. It has no title, and follows the Hymn to Åmen immediately, beginning with the words, " Homage to thee, ÅTEN of the day ! " He is called " creator of men and women, maker of their lives," and is identified with the " Great Hawk of many-coloured plumage." He performed the act of creation which " raised " himself up [out of the primeval watery abyss]. " The creator of himself he was not born." He is next identified with the " Aged Horus," the dweller in Nut, the oldest solar god or sky-god in Egypt, and is acclaimed joyfully at rising and setting. He created the earth (?). The next words, *Khnem Amen Ḥenmemit,* are difficult. If the writer of the hymn meant to identify Åten with Khnem-Åmen, a god of the region of the First Cataract, that is understandable, but how, then, is Ḥenmemit, if that be the correct reading, to be fitted in ? [1] Åten is next called " Conqueror of the Two Lands from the greatest to the least." Another difficulty meets us in the words " glorious mother of gods and men," and the words that follow, " gracious artificer, most great, prospering in her work," seem to apply to this mother. Perhaps the writer of the hymn wished to compare Åten to such a mother, or he may have regarded Åten

[1] The true reading may be ***hememit*** and so be connected with the word to " roar "—Khnem Åmen of the roarings. Åmenḥetep IV dedicated a scarab to a god of roarings (British Museum, No. 51084).

as father-mother. After another line containing obscure allusions we read, "How marvellous is production of him who raises up his beauty from the womb of Nut, and who illumines the Two Lands with his Āten (Disk)! He the Pautti (the primeval matter out of which the world and all in it were made) created himself. He is the LORD ONE. He made the Seasons out of the

Ḥer-netch-tef-f, or Horus the Avenger of his Father.

Ḥer-āakhuti as Ment, or Menthu, the War-god of Hermonthis.

months, Summer because he loves heat, and Winter because he loves the cold; [during the former] he makes men's bodies to become exhausted. The apes sing hymns to him when he rises daily." What follows on the stele concerns the lives of Ḥer and Suti, and the text is translated on pp. 46–68.

Judging by what is said in the Hymn to Āten,

the origin, nature and attributes of Åten closely resemble those of Åmen. Both gods are identified with the oldest gods in Egypt. Each is declared to be self-created and not to have been born, therefore not begotten, and to each is applied the epithet "ONE." It is interesting to note that Åten is identified with Pautti, the oldest of all the gods, and with the Aged Horus, or Horus the Elder. As Åten is said to be the maker of Summer and Winter and the months, it is clear that a tradition, probably going back to predynastic times, associated him with the primitive Year-god. This Hymn shows that our two architects regarded Åten as a thoroughly Egyptian god, and as one who could be and ought to be worshipped side by side with Åmen, who had condescended to become the begetter of their lord and master, Åmenḥetep III.

Notwithstanding the influence of his mother, the Mitannian princess, and of his wives, some of whom also came from Mitanni, Åmenḥetep strongly supported the cult of Åmen throughout the country, and kept on good terms with the priesthood of Åmen. The consolidation of that order by Thothmes III has already been mentioned, and it would seem that this king instituted, or, at all events, sanctioned the daily performance of a very important service in the sanctuary of Åmen in the temple of Karnak. In the sanctuary there was placed a naos, or shrine, containing a gold or gilded wooden figure of Åmen, with moveable head, arms and legs; sometimes a boat took the place of the shrine, and in such cases the figure of the god was set inside the cabin. The figure might represent the god standing upright or seated on a throne. During the service the king, or his deputy, purified the sanctuary and himself by burning incense and pouring out

Head of a colossal statue of Åmenḥetep III, wearing the uraeus, the symbol of sovereignty, above his forehead. Found by Mr. H. Salt during the excavations which he made near the Colossi in Western Thebes.
British Museum, Northern Egyptian Gallery.

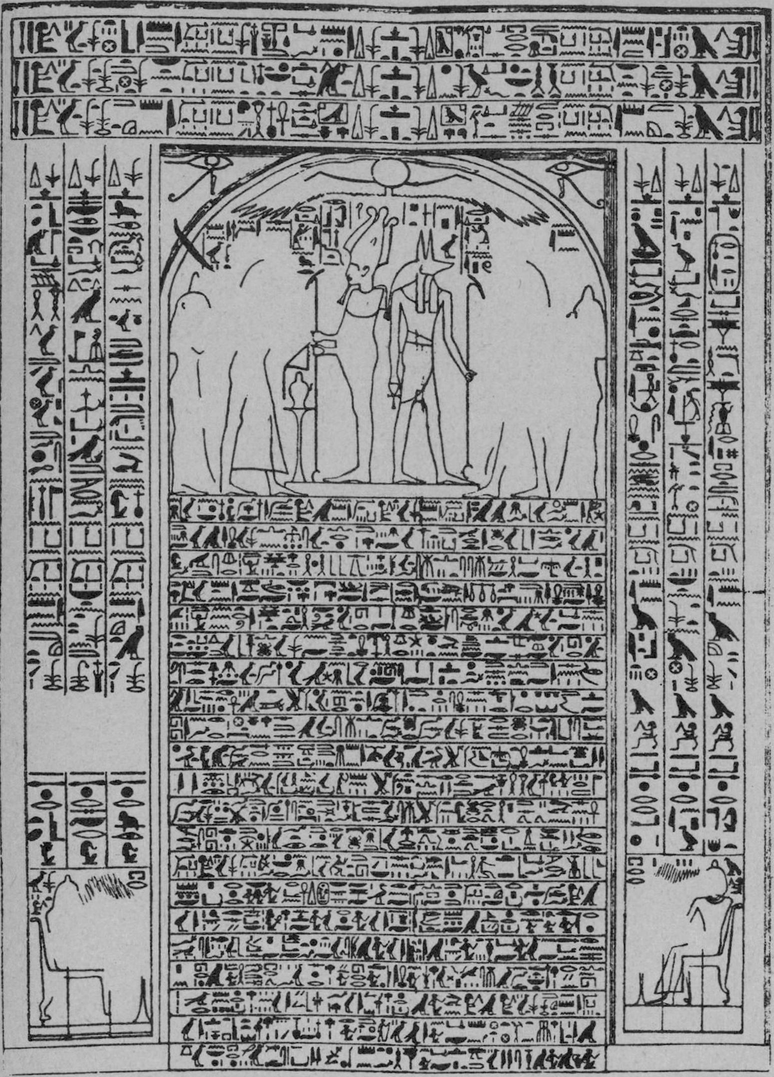

Stele of Ḥer and Suti, twin brothers who were overseers of the works of Ȧmen-ḥetep III at Thebes. The text contains a Hymn to Ȧmen, and a Hymn to Ȧten.
British Museum, No. 475.

libations of fresh water. He then advanced to the naos, broke the seal which closed its doors, and made obeisance to the figure of the god. Having performed further rites of purification on the figure, he advanced and embraced it, in order that the soul of the god might enter into his body. The naos was closed, and the king left the sanctuary, but he returned immediately, when the naos was reopened, and he performed further acts of obeisance, and made offerings which included a figure of the goddess Maāt , or TRUTH. Next the king dressed the figure in symbolic garments, and purified it, and anointed it with scented unguents and perfumes, and placed on it a necklace, amulets, rings, etc. By these acts the king intended to imply that he, the son of a god, was adoring his father, just as children in general adore their fathers and mothers in the tomb. During some of these ceremonies the god laid his hands on the body of the king, and by so doing transmitted to him the fluid of life, which enabled the king to live day by day, and to rule over his people with wisdom and justice. Now the king himself might well perform his part in this great, solemn service at Thebes, but he could not be at the same time at Abydos or elsewhere in Egypt. Therefore in Thebes and other cities deputies were chosen to represent the king, and they were everywhere regarded with the reverence that was due to the performers of such exalted duties. During the performance of these rites and ceremonies hymns were chanted to Āmen or Āmen-Rā, and of these the following are specimens :[1]—

[1] A hieroglyphic transcript of the hieratic text will be found in Moret, *Le Rituel du Culte Divin Journalier en Égypte*, Paris, 1902, p. 69.

I. " Homage to thee, O Åmen-Rā, Lord of Thebes,
Thou Boy, the ornament of the gods !
All men lift up their faces to gaze upon him.
Thou art the Lord, inspiring awe, crushing those who would revolt [against thee].
Thou art the King of all the gods.
Thou art the great god, the Living One.

Menu Ka-mut-f, or Menu, Bull of his mother, a god of new birth and virility, with whom Åmen and Åmen-Rā were identified.

Thou art beloved for thy words,
[Which are] the satisfaction of the gods.
Thou art the King of heaven, thou didst make the stars.
Thou art the *tchām* metal (gold) of the gods (*i.e.*, the gold out of which the gods are made).

Thou art the Maker of heaven, thou didst open the horizon and make the gods to come into being according to thy behests.

[O] Āmen-Rā, Lord of the Throne of the Two Lands, President of the Āpit, Āmen-Rā, Bull of his mother, who art upon thy great throne, Lord of rays, Maker of multitudes, god of the lofty plumes, thou art the King of the gods, the Great Hawk, who makest the breast to rejoice. Thou art praised by all rational beings [because] they have life."

II. "Watch, being at peace! Thou watchest in peace. Watch, Āmen-Rā, Lord of the Throne of the Two Lands, in peace.

Watch, being at peace! Thou watchest in peace. Watch, Chief in On, Great One in Thebes, in peace.

Watch, being at peace! Thou watchest in peace. Watch, Creator of the Two Lands (Egypt), in peace.

Watch, being at peace! Thou watchest in peace. Watch, thou who didst build up thyself, in peace.

Watch, being at peace! Thou watchest in peace. Watch, Creator of heaven and the hidden things of the two horizons, in peace.

Watch, being at peace! Thou watchest in peace. Watch, O thou to whom the gods come with bowings, Lord who art feared,

Mighty One whom the hearts of all rational beings hold in awe, in peace." (*Ibid.*, p. 122.)

III. "Image of the Eldest Son, Heir of the earth before thy father the Earth [Geb and] thy mother Nut, Divine Image, who camest into being in primeval time, , when a god did not exist, and when the name of nothing whatsoever had been recorded, when thou didst open thy two eyes and didst look out of them light appeared unto every man. When shadow is pleasing to thy two eyes, day exists no longer.

Thou openest thy mouth, thy word is therein.

Geb, the Earth-god, Father of the Gods, Great God, Lord of Eternity.

Nut, the Sky-goddess, the Lady of Heaven, who gave birth to Osiris and Isis and Set and Nephthys.

Thou stablishest heaven with thy two arms, and the West (*ȧment*) in thy name of Ȧmen.

Thou art the Image of the Ka (or Double) of all the gods, Image of Ȧmen, Image of Ȧtem, Image of Kheperȧ, Image of the Lord of all the earth, Image of the Lord who is crowned King of the South and North in the North and South, Image who gavest birth to the gods, who gavest birth to men, who gavest birth to everything, the Lord of life, thou Living One, who possessest power greater than that of all the gods. Thou hast conquered the Nine Gods, thou hast presented to them their offering. Thou hast bound them together, thou hast made them to live. O thou Image who hast created their doubles (?), thou hast

Ptaḥ, lord of Maāt, king of the Two Lands (Egypt), the great Man-god of Memphis.

Sekhmit, the great lady, the lady of heaven, the mistress of the Two Lands (Egypt). She was a female counterpart of Ptaḥ.

given that which Horus has obtained for himself from the Company of the gods. Thou art like a god who designs with thy fingers, like a god who designs with thy toes. Thou hast become the Lord of everything, Åten who came into being in primeval time, god of the two high plumes. Thou Begetter, thou hast created more than all the gods." (*Ibid.*, p. 129.)

A papyrus at Leyden contains a series of very interesting hymns to Åmen, and the following extracts are quoted from it.

IV. "' Thou sailest, Ḥeråakhuti, and each day thou dost fulfil the behest of yesterday. Thou art the maker of the years and captain of the months; days and nights and hours are according to his stride. Thou makest thyself new to-day for yesterday; though going in as the night thou art the day. The One Watcher, he hates slumber. Men sleep on their beds, but his eyes watch. (Chap. VI.)

Fashioning himself none knows his forms. (Chap. VIII.)

Mingling his seed with his body to make his egg to come into being within himself. (Chap. VIII.)

The Åten (Disk) of heaven, his rays are on thy face.

He drove out the Nile from his cavern for thy Pautti. The earth is made thy statue 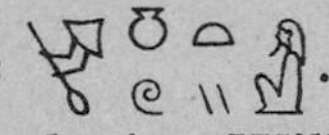. Thy name is victorious, thy souls (or Will) are weighty.

Hawk destroying his attacker straightway. Hidden (or secret) Lion roaring loudly, driving his claws into what is under his paws, Bull for his town, Lion for his people. The earth shakes when he sends forth his voice. Every being is in awe of him, mighty in power there is none like him. He is the Beneficent Power of the births of the Nine gods. (Chap. IX.)

Loosing evils, driving away sicknesses. A physician healing the eye without medicines; Opener of the eye, destroyer of the cast in it. Being in the Tuat he releases him whom he loves. Removing from Destiny according to his heart's desire. Possessing eyes and ears he is on every path of him that loves him.

He hears the petitions of him that invokes him. Being afar off he comes in a moment to him that calls him.

He adds to the term of life and he shortens it.

To him whom he loves he gives more than Fate has allotted to him.

To the man who sets him in his heart he is more than millions.

With his name one man is stronger than hundreds of thousands. (Chap. XI.)

Thou didst exist first in the forms of the Eight Gods [of Hermopolis], and then thou didst complete them and become ONE, .

Thy body is hidden in the Chiefs, thou art hidden as Ȧmen at the head of the gods.

Thy form was that of Tanen in order to give birth to the Pautti gods in thy primeval matter. Thou dost enter fathers making their sons. Thou didst first come into being when there was no being in existence. All the gods came into being after thee. (Chap. XIII.)

Ȧmen came into being in primeval time, none knows the form in which he appeared. No god existed before him, there was no other god with him to declare his form.

He had no mother for whom his name was made. He had no father who begot him, saying, It is even myself. He shaped his own egg; the divine god, becoming of himself; all the gods were created after he came into being. (Chap. XIV.)

One is Åmen, he hides himself from them, he conceals himself from the gods.

The man who utters his secret (or mystery) name, which cannot be known, falls down upon his face straightway and dies a violent death. No god knows how to call upon him." (Chap. XV.)[1]

The extracts given in the last section are taken from a work on Åmen which was not intended to be sung in the temples. It is, more or less, a philosophical treatise on the origin, nature, and powers of the god, showing that he is the source of all life, animate and inanimate. The existence of other gods is admitted, but they are merely forms of him, the great god whose three characters or persons were called Åmen (of Thebes), Rā (of Heliopolis) and Ptaḥ (of Memphis). His ONENESS, or Unity, was absolute. We may now give an extract from the famous Hymn to Åmen which is preserved in a papyrus in the Egyptian Museum, Cairo,[2] and was undoubtedly sung by men and women to the accompaniment of music in the temples.

[1] For transcripts of the hieratic texts, translations, etc., see Gardiner in *Aegyptische Zeitschrift*, Bd. 42 (1905), p. 12 ff.

[2] A complete transcript of the hieratic text into hieroglyphs, with a French translation, has been published by Grébaut, *Hymne à Ammon-Ra*, Paris, 1875.

A Hymn to Āmen-Rā.

§I. Bull, dwelling in On, President of all the gods,
Beautiful god, Meriti (he who is loved),
Giving all life of warmth
To all beautiful cattle.

§II. Hail to thee, Āmen-Rā, Lord of the Throne of the Two Lands!
First One in the Āpts (*i.e.*, Karnak),
Bull of his mother, first one of his pasture,
Extended of stride, first one of the Land of the South,
Lord of the Matchaiu (Nubians), Governor of Punt,
Prince of Heaven, Eldest one of Earth,
Lord of things which are, stablisher of creation, stablisher of all creation.

§III. One, through his unrivalled powers among the gods, Chief of all the gods,
Lord of Truth, Father of the gods,
Maker of men, creator of beasts,
Lord of the things that are, creator of the plant of life (wheat),
Maker of green plants, making to live the cattle.

§IV. Power, produced by Ptaḥ,
Beautiful Boy of love,
The gods ascribe praises to him,
Maker of things below and of things above, illumining Egypt,
Sailing over the heavens in peace.
King of the South and North (Rā),
Whose word is true, Chief of the Two Lands (Egypt),

Great of power, Lord of awe,
Chief, making the earth like his form,
Dispenser of destinies (or plans) more
than any god.

§IX. Casting down his enemy into the flame,
His eye overthroweth the Sebȧu fiends.
It maketh her spear stab Nun (the
abyss of heaven),
It maketh the serpent fiend Nȧk vomit
what he hath swallowed.

§X. Hail to thee, Rā, Lord of Truth !
Hidden one in his shrine, Lord of the
gods,
Kheperȧ in his boat.
He sent out the Word, the gods came
into being,
Temu, maker of men,
Making different their characters and
forms, making their life,
Distinguishing by their skins one from
the other.

§XI. He hearkeneth to the groan of the
afflicted,
Being gracious to him that crieth to
him,
Delivering the timid man from the
bully.
Judging between the oppressor and the
helpless one.

§XV. Image One, 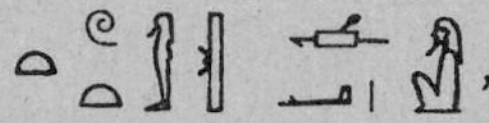, maker of
everything that is,
One Alone, 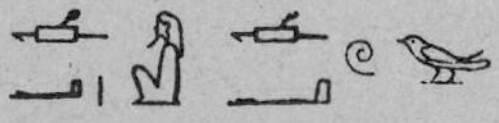, maker of
things that are.

Men proceed from his eyes,
The gods come into being by his utterance;
Maker of green herbs, Vivifier of the cattle,
The staff of life of the Henmemet beings,
Making the fish to live in the river,
And the geese in the sky,
Giving air to the creature in the egg,
Making to live feathered fowl,
Making *khennur* birds to live,
And creeping things and insects likewise,
Providing food for the mice in their holes,
And making the birds to live on every branch.

§XIX. Chief of the Great Nine Gods,
ONE ALONE, without a second 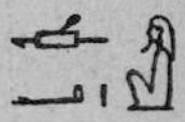

A HYMN TO ÅMEN AND ÅTEN

BY

ḤER AND SUTI, OVERSEERS OF WORKS AT THEBES, IN THE REIGN OF ÅMENḤETEP III.

[British Museum, Stele No. 475.[1]]

1. 

2. 

1. A Hymn of Praise to Åmen when he riseth as Horus of the Two Horizons by Suti, the Overseer of the Works of Åmen, [and by] Ḥer (Horus), the Overseer of the Works of Åmen. They say:—Homage to thee, Rā, Beautiful (or Beneficent) One of every day! Thou shootest up

2. at sunrise (or dawn) without fail,[2] Kheperå,[3]

[1] This monument has been published by Pierret, *Recueil*, tome I., p. 20 and by Birch, *Trans. Soc. Bibl. Arch.*, Vol. VIII, p. 143 ff.

[2] Literally, "he maketh not cessation."

[3] Or "Creator." Here Åmen is identified with the ancient god of Creation.

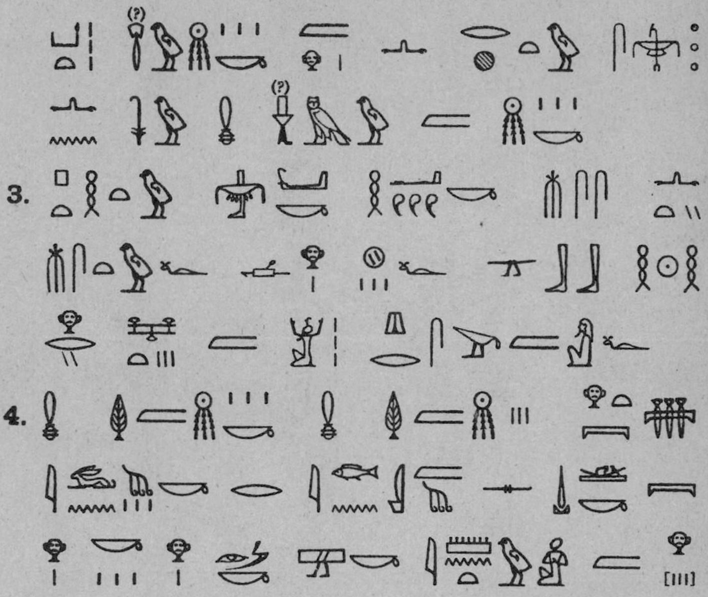

great one of works. Thy radiance is in thy face, [thou] Unknown. [As for] shining metal[1] it doth not resemble thy splendours.

3. Being designed[2] thou didst mould into form thy members ; giving birth, but he was not born ; One by himself by reason of his power (or abilities), Traverser of Eternity, He who is over (or Chief of) the ways of millions of years, maintaining his Divine Form.

4. As are the beauties of the celestial regions even so are thy beauties. More brilliant is thy complexion than that of heaven. Thou sailest across the heavens, all faces (*i.e.*, mankind) look at thee as thou goest, though thou thyself art hidden from their faces.

[1] *Tchām*, perhaps gilded copper, or even gold itself. The caps of the obelisks were covered with it.

[2] Meaning perhaps, " thou didst design thine own form."

5. 

6. 

7. 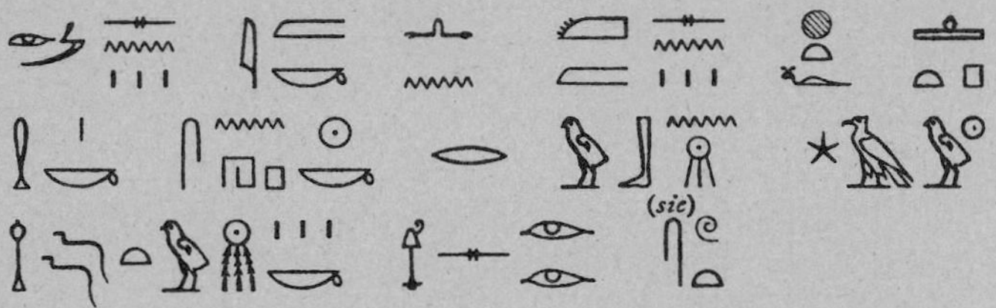

5. Thou showest thyself at break of day in beams of light, strong is thy Seqeṭ Boat under Thy Majesty. In a little day thou journeyest over a road of millions and hundreds of thousands

6. of minutes (or moments). Thy (?) day with thee passeth, [thou] settest.

The hours of the night likewise thou dost make to fulfil themselves. No interruption taketh place in thy toil. All eyes (*i.e.*, mankind, or all peoples)

7. direct their gaze upon thee, they cease not to do so. When Thy Majesty setteth, thou makest haste (?) to rise up early in the morning,[1] thy sparkling rays flash in the eyes (or penetrate the eyes).

[1] The text is probably corrupt here; the writer meant to say "When Thy Majesty setteth, thou shinest and risest upon the Ṭuat" (the Underworld).

8. 

9. 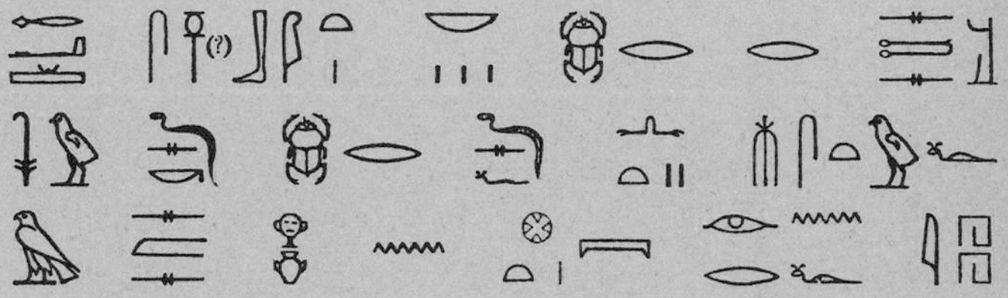

10. 

8. Thou settest in Manu, whereupon [men] sleep after the manner of the dead.

Hail to thee, O ÅTEN of the day, thou Creator of mortals [and] Maker of their life (*i.e.*, that on which they live)! [Hail]

9. thou Great Hawk whose feathers are many-coloured, thou god Kheprer, who didst raise thyself up [from non-existence]! He created himself, he was not born, Horus the Elder (or the Old Hawk), dweller in Nut (the sky). [Men] cry out joyfully at

10. his rising [and] at his setting likewise. [He is] the fashioner [of what] the ground produceth, Khnem Åmen of the Henmemet,[1] conqueror of the Two Lands, from the great one to the little one. [Thou] Mother splendid of

[1] A class of celestial beings.

11. 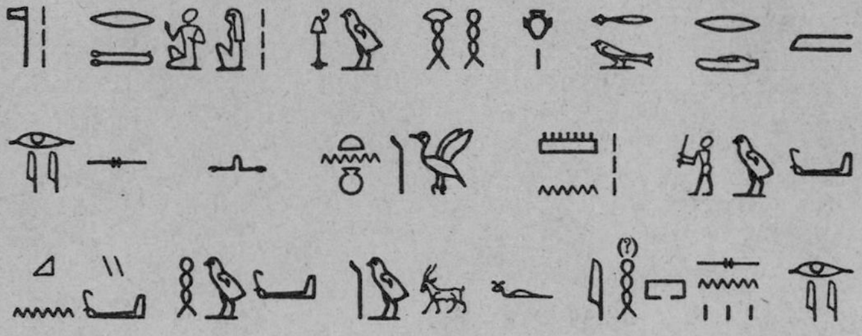

12. 

11. Gods and men, artificer, gracious one, exceedingly great, progressing (or flourishing) in her work. The cattle (?) cannot be counted. The strong herdsman, driving his strong beasts, thou art their byre. He

12. provideth their life (*i.e.*, sustenance), springing up, traversing the course (?) of Kheperȧ, planning (?) his birth, raising up his beautiful [form] in the womb of Nut. He illumineth the Two Lands (Egypt) with his Ȧten (or Disk), [he is] the primeval substance (or plasma) of the Two Lands. He made himself.

13. 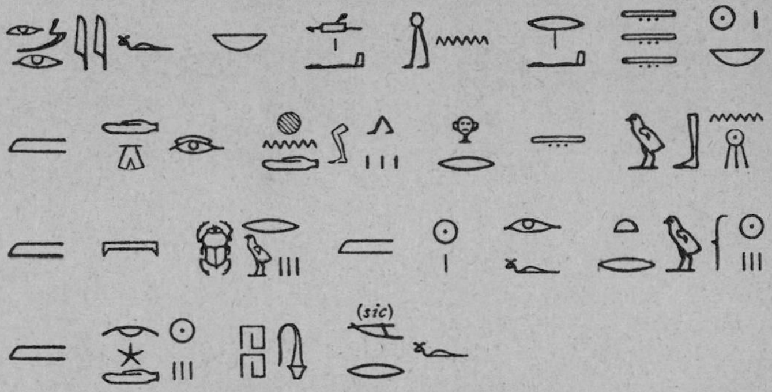

14. 

13. He looketh on what he hath made, the Lord ONE, bringing along into captivity countless lands every day, observing those who walk about upon the earth; shining (or shooting up) in the sky [he performeth] transformations by day (or, as Rā). He maketh the seasons from the months. He loveth the heat of summer.

14. He loveth the cold of winter. He maketh every member of the body to droop. He embraceth every land. The ape[s cry out] in adoration of him when he riseth daily.

15. 

16. 

15. Suti, overseer of works, [and] Ḥer, overseer of works, [each] saith, "I was the director of thy throne [and] overseer of works in thy sanctuary [which], as was right, thy beloved son, the Lord of the Two Lands, Nebmaātrā, the giver of life, made for thee. My Lord appointed me to be the officer in charge of thy monuments.

16. I kept watch diligently, I served the office of director of thy monuments strenuously, performing the laws of thy heart. I knew how to make thee to rest upon Truth, making thee great to do it upon the earth.

17. 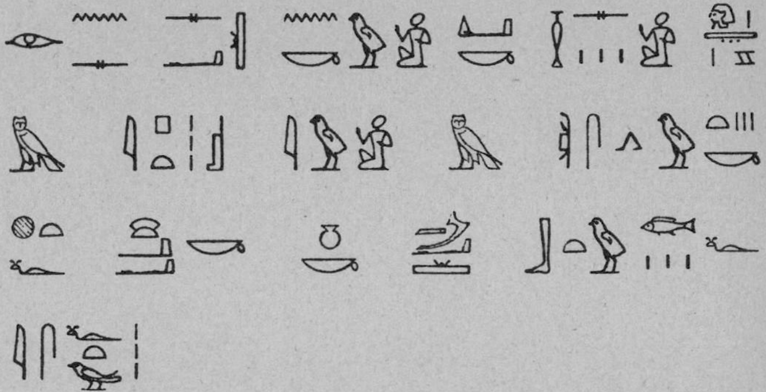

18. 

17. I was performing it [and] thou didst make me great. Thou didst set the favours [or praises] of me on the earth in the Åpts (Karnak). I was among thy followers when thou didst ascend the throne. I am truth who abominateth false words and deeds.

18. I never took pleasure in any conversation wherein were words of exaggeration and lies. My brother was like myself. I took pleasure in his affairs ; he came forth from the womb with me on this (*i.e.*, the same) day.

19. 

20. 

21. 

19. Suti, the overseer of the works of Åmen in the Southern Åpt (*i.e.*, Luxor), and Ḥer [the overseer of works], say:—I was director over the western side, and he was director over the eastern side; we two were directors of the great monuments

20. in the Åpt, more particularly those of Thebes, the City of Åmen. Grant thou to me an old age in thy city, and in thy beneficence make me a burial in Åmentt, that place of rest of heart.

21. Let me be placed among thy favoured ones, departing in peace. Grant thou to me sweet air when . . . . [and] the wearing (or bearing) of bandlets on the day of the festival of Ug.

THE CULT OF ÅTEN, THE GOD AND DISK OF THE SUN, ITS ORIGIN, DEVELOPMENT AND DECLINE.

Amongst all the mass of the religious literature of Ancient Egypt, there is no document that may be considered to contain a reasoned and connected account of the ideas and beliefs which the Egyptians associated with the god Åten. The causes of his rise into favour towards the close of the XVIIIth dynasty can be surmised, and the principal dogmas which the founder of his cult and his followers promulgated are discoverable in the Hymns that are found on the walls of the rock-hewn tombs of Tall al-'Amârnah; but the true history of the rise, development and fall of the cult can never be completely known. The word *åten*,  or *åthen* 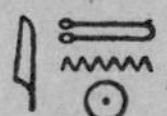, is a very old word for the "disk" or "face of the sun," and Åtenism was beyond doubt an old form of worship of the sun. But there were many forms of sun-worship older than the cult of Åten, and several solar gods were worshipped in Egypt many, many centuries before Åten was regarded as a special form of the great solar god at all. One of the oldest forms of the Sun-god worshipped in Egypt was ḤER (Horus), who in the earliest times seems to have represented the "height" or "face" of heaven by day. He was symbolized by the sparrowhawk , the right eye of the bird representing the sun and his left the moon.

In later times he was called " Ḥer-ur " or " Ḥer-sems," the " older Horus," and it was he who fought daily against Set, the darkness of night and the night sky, and triumphed over him.

The oldest seat of the cult of the Sun-god was the famous city of Ānu , the On of the Bible, and the Heliopolis of Greek and Latin writers.

Horus, hawk-headed, and Set, his twin brother; the former was god of the day, and the latter god of the night.

The goddess Nephthys who, according to Heliopolitan Theology, was a female counterpart of Set.

Here, from time immemorial, existed a temple dedicated to the Sun-god, and attached to it was a college of his priests, who from a very remote period were renowned for their wisdom and learning. They called their god TEM or ĀTEM 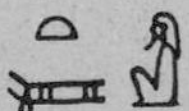, , and in later times, at least, he was depicted in the form of a man wearing the Crowns of the South and North, and holding in his right hand *ānkh* ☥ ("life") and in his left a sceptre. He was king of heaven and also of Egypt. He was a solar god and, like every other ancient god in Egypt, had absorbed the attributes of several indigenous gods whose names even

Shu, son of Rā, source of heat and light.

Tefnut, daughter of Rā, source of moisture and water. She was a female counterpart of Shu.

are now not known. The Pyramid Texts show that he was all-powerful in heaven, and that his priests proclaimed him to be the greatest of all the gods. The supremacy of Tem is asserted in the various versions of the Book of the Dead, and all the other solar gods are regarded as forms of him in the various recensions of this work. Thus in the XVIIth Chapter he says: "I am Tem in his rising. I was the Only One [when] I came into existence in Nenu (or Nu). I am Rā when he rose for the first time. I am the Great God who created himself [from] Nenu, and who made his names to become the gods of his company. I am he who is irresistible among the gods. I am Tem, the dweller in his Disk 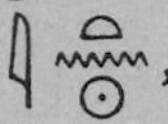, or Rā in his rising in the eastern horizon of the sky. I am Yesterday; I know To-day. I am the Bennu (*i.e.*, Phœnix) which is in Ȧnu (Heliopolis), and I keep the register of the things which are created and of those which are not yet in existence." The Company of the gods over whom "Father Tem" presided consisted of Shu and Tefnut, Geb and Nut, Osiris and Isis, and Set and Nephthys. According to one tradition, Tem produced Shu and Tefnut from his own body, and these three gods formed the first Triad, or Trinity, Tem saying, "From [being] god one I became three."

In the extract from the XVIIth Chapter given above, we must note that 1. Tem originally existed in Nenu, or Nu, the great mass of primeval waters. 2. He was the Only One in existence when he had come into being. 3. He created himself the Great God. 4. He possessed various names, and these he turned into the gods who formed his Pest or Ennead, merely by uttering their names. 5. He was irresistible among the gods, *i.e.*, he was the Over-lord of the gods. 6. He comprehended time past and time to come. 7. He dwelt in the Solar Disk (Ȧten). 8. He rose in the sky for the first time under the form of Rā, and he was himself the Bennu, *i.e.*, the Soul of Rā. 9. He kept the Registers of things created and uncreated. Though the papyrus from which we get these facts is not older than the XVIIIth dynasty, each of the statements which are here grouped exists in the various religious texts that were written under the Ancient Empire, say, two thousand years earlier.

Of the style and nature of the worship of Tem we know nothing, but, from the fact that he was depicted in the form of a man, we appear to be justified in assuming that it was of a character

Osiris, Lord of Eternity, Bull of Åmentt.

Isis, female counterpart of Osiris, and mother of Horus.

superior to that of the cults of sacred animals, birds and reptiles, which were general in Egypt under the earlier dynasties. Tem, the man-god, absorbed the attributes of Ḥer-ur, the old Sky-god, and of Kheperå, the Beetle-god, who represented one or more of the forms of an ancient Sun-god between sunset and sunrise, and of Ḥer-åakhuti ("Horus of the two horizons"). Kheperå was the sun during the hour that precedes the dawn. Ḥer was the sun by day, and Tem was the setting sun; the names of these gods are of native origin. We may conclude that the priests of Tem incorporated into their forms of worship as many as possible of the rites and ceremonies to which the people had been accustomed in their worship of the older gods. For there was nothing strange in the absorption of one god by another to the Egyptian, the god absorbed being regarded by him merely as a phase or character of the absorbing god. The Egyptians, like many other Orientals, were exceedingly tolerant in such matters.

The monuments prove that, quite early in the Dynastic Period, there was known and worshipped in Lower Egypt another form of the Sun-god who was called Rā 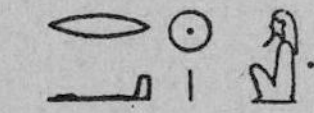. Of his origin and early history nothing is known, and the meaning of his name has not yet been satisfactorily explained. It does not seem to be Egyptian, but it may be that of some Asiatic sun-god, whose cult was introduced into Egypt at a very remote period. His character and attributes closely resemble those of the Babylonian god Marduk, and both Rā and Marduk may be only different names of one and the same ancestor. The centre of the cult of Rā in Egypt was Ȧnu, or Heliopolis, and the city must have been inhabited by a cosmopolitan population (who were chiefly worshippers of the sun) from time immemorial. All the caravans from Arabia and Syria halted there, whether outward or homeward bound, and men of many nations and tongues must have exchanged ideas there as well as commodities. The control of the water drawn from the famous Well of the Sun, the 'Ain ash-Shams' of Arab writers, was, no doubt, in the hands of the priests of Ȧnu, and the payments made by grateful travellers for the watering of their beasts, together with other offerings, made them rich and powerful. The waters of the well were believed to spring from the celestial waters of Nenu, or Nu, and the Nubian King Piānkhi tells us that when he went to Ånu he bathed his face in the water in which Rā was wont to bathe his face.[1] We may note in passing that the Virgin Mary drew water from this well when the Holy Family halted at Ånu.

Under the IVth dynasty the priests of Ånu obtained very considerable power, and they succeeded in acquiring pre-eminence for their god Rā among the other gods of Lower Egypt. Whether or not they chose the kings cannot be said, but it is certain that they caused the name of Rā to form a part of the Nesu båt names of the builders of the second and third pyramids at Gîzah. Thus we have KHĀF-RĀ (Khephren) and MENKAU-RĀ (Mycerinus). Not satisfied with this, they rejected the descendants of the great pyramid builders, and set upon the throne a number of kings whom they declared to be the sons of their god Rā by the wife of one of his priests. The first of these adopted as his fifth, or personal name, the title of "Sa Rā," *i.e.*, son of Rā. This title, which was certainly adopted by the kings of the Vth dynasty, was borne by every king of Egypt afterwards, and the Nubian, Persian, Macedonian, or Roman who became king of Egypt saw no absurdity in styling himself "son of Rā." Thanks to the excavations made by Borchardt and Schäfer, under the direction of F. von Bissing, several important facts dealing with the worship of Rā have been brought to light. The sun temples built by the later kings of the Vth dynasty were usually buildings

[1] Stele of Piānkhi, l. 102.

about 325 feet long and 245 feet broad. At the west end stood a truncated, or "blunted," pyramid (A), and on the top of it was an obelisk made of stone (B). In front of the east side of the pyramid stood an alabaster altar, and on the north side of the altar were channels along which the blood of the victims, both animal and human, ran into alabaster bowls which were placed to receive it. On the north side of the rectangular walled enclosure was a row of store rooms, and on the east and south sides were passages, the walls of which were decorated with reliefs. Opposite the altar, on the east side, was a gateway; from this ran a path, which led by an inclined causeway to another gate, which formed the entrance to another large enclosure, about 1,000 feet square. The priests lived in this enclosure, and in special chambers were kept the sacred objects which were carried in procession on days of festival.

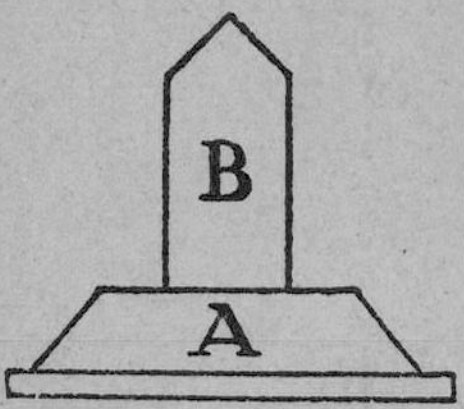

The principal object of the cult of Rā and his special symbol was the obelisk, but it has been suggested that the earliest worshippers of the sun believed that their god dwelt in a particular stone of pyramidal shape. At stated seasons, or for special purposes, the Spirit of the Sun was induced by the priests to inhabit the stone, and it was believed to be present when gifts were offered up to the god, and when human victims, who were generally prisoners of war, were sacrificed. The exact signification of this sun symbol is not known. Some think that the obelisk represented the axis of earth and heaven, but the Egyptians can hardly have evolved such an idea; others assign to it a phallic signification, and others associate it with an object that produced fire and heat. That it symbolized Rā is certain, and there was in every sanctuary a shrine in which, behind sealed doors, was a model of an obelisk. The cult of the standing stone, or pillar, was probably older than the cult of Rā, and the old name of Heliopolis is Ânu, , *i.e.*, the city of the pillar. The Spirit of the Sun

Osiris Khenti Âmentt, god and judge of the dead and lord of the Other World.

The triune god of the Osirian Resurrection. The three members of his triad were Seker, an old Death-god of Memphis; Ptaḥ, a Creation-god of Memphis; and Osiris, the vivifier of the dead.

visited the temple of the sun from time to time in the form of a Bennu bird, and alighted "on the Ben-stone,[1] in the house of the Bennu in Ânu"; in later times the Bennu-bird, which

[1] , Pyramid Texts, II. N. 663, p. 372.

the Egyptians regarded as the "soul of Rā," was known as the Phoinix, or Phœnix.

Under the VIth dynasty the priests of Rā succeeded in thrusting their god into the position of over-lord of all the gods, and as we see from the names Rā-Kheperȧ, Rā-Ȧtem, Rā-Ḥer-ȧakhuti and the like, all the old solar gods of the north of Egypt were regarded as forms of Rā. He was king of heaven and judge of gods and men, and the attempt was also made to make the people accept him as the over-lord of Osiris and king of the Tuat, or Underworld. But in this last matter the priests failed, and Osiris maintained his position as the god and judge of the dead. The priests had assigned to Rā in the funerary compositions, which are now known as the "Pyramid Texts," great powers over the dead, and, in fact, over all the gods and demons and denizens of the underworld, but before a century had passed, Osiris had established absolute sovereignty over his realm of Ȧmentt.

From what has been said above it is evident that, before the close of the VIth dynasty, the priests of the various solar gods of Lower Egypt had assigned to each of them all the essential powers and characteristics which Ȧmenḥetep claimed for his god Ȧten. But before we consider these powers in detail we must summarize briefly the principal historical facts relating to the rise and development of the Ȧten cult. Wherever a solar god was worshipped in Egypt the habitat of this god was believed to be the solar Disk (*ȧten* 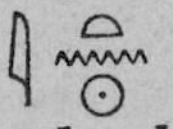 or *ȧthen* ). But the oldest solar god who was associated with the Disk was Tem, or Ȧtmu, who is frequently referred to in religious texts as "Tem in his Disk"; when Rā usurped the attributes of Tem he became the "dweller in his Disk." Ḥerȧakhuti was the "god of the two horizons," *i.e.*, the Sun-god by day, from sunrise to sunset, and in the hieroglyphs with which his name is written , we see the Disk resting upon the horizon of the east and the horizon of the west. Thothmes IV, who owed his throne to the priesthoods of Tem and Rā at Heliopolis, incorporated the name of Tem in his Nebti title, and styled himself "made of Rā," "chosen of Rā," and "beloved of Rā." As the name of Ȧmen is wanting in every one of his titles, it seems reasonable to assume that his personal sympathies lay with the cult of the solar gods of the North and not with the cult of Ȧmen of Thebes. But he maintained good relations with the priests of Ȧmen, and made gifts to their god, who through the victories of Thothmes III was recognized in the Egyptian Sûdân, Egypt, and Syria as the god of all the world.

Thothmes IV was succeeded by his son Ȧmenḥetep, the third king to bear the name, and the priesthood of Thebes asserted that he was the veritable son of their god Ȧmen, whose blood ran in his veins. According to this fiction the god assumed the form of Thothmes IV, and Queen Mutemuȧa became with child by him. How much or how little religious instruction the child received cannot be said, but it is probable that any teaching which he received from his mother, the princess of Mitanni, would make his mind to incline towards the religion of her native land. From the titles which Ȧmenḥetep assumed when he became king it is clear that he was content to be "the chosen of Rā," "the chosen of Tem," or "the chosen of Ȧmen," and it seems to have mattered little to him whether he was the "beloved" and

"emanation of Rā" or the "beloved" and "emanation of Åmen." His predecessors on the throne of Egypt believed in all seriousness that they had divine blood in their veins, and they acted as they thought gods would act; they had themselves hedged round with elaborate ceremonial procedure, which made men believe that their king was a god. To Åmenḥetep all the gods of Egypt were alike, and we see from the bas-reliefs in the temple at Sulb, some fifty miles above the head of the Second Cataract, that he was as willing to worship himself and to offer sacrifices to himself as to Åmen, in whose honour he had rebuilt the temple. It is impossible to think of his performing daily the rites and ceremonies which the king of Egypt was expected to perform in the shrine of Åmen-Rā at Karnak, in order to obtain from the god the power and knowledge necessary for governing his people.

One of the most important events in his life, and one fraught with very far-reaching consequences, was his marriage with the lady Ti (or Teî) 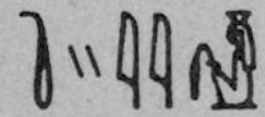, a private individual, apparently of no high rank or social position.[1] In the Tall al-'Amârnah letters her name is transcribed Teî 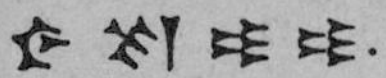. Her father was called Iuâu  and her mother Thuâu . Their tomb was discovered in 1905,[2] and it is clear that before the marriage of their daughter to Åmenḥetep III they were humble folk. According to a consensus of modern Egyptological opinion they were natives of Egypt, not foreigners as the older Egyptologists supposed. Be this as it may, there is no doubt that Ti was

[1] See Davis, *The Tomb of Queen Tîyi*, London, 1910.
[2] See Davis, *Tomb of Iouiya and Touiyou*, London, 1907.

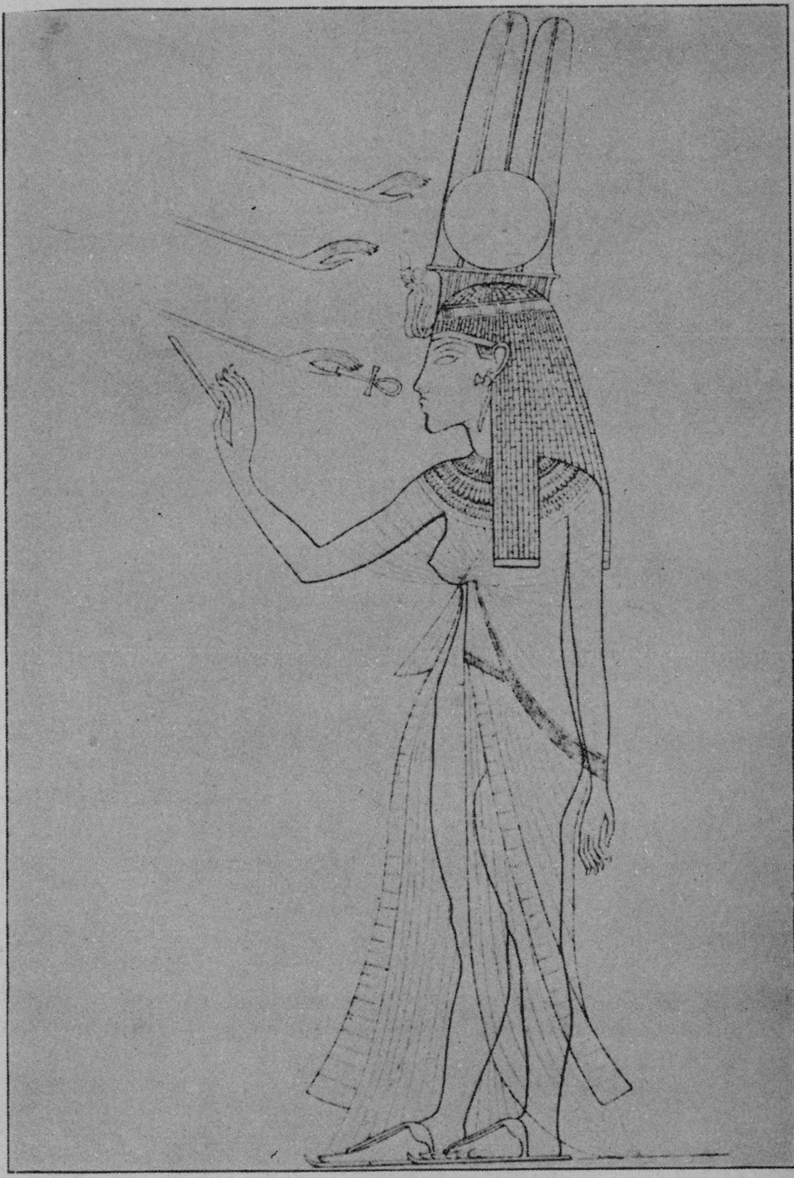

Queen Ti, wife of Ȧmenḥetep III. From a drawing in Davis's work on her tomb (Plate XXXIII).

Large steatite scarab recording the slaughter of two hundred and twenty-six wild cattle by Ȧmenḥetep III. British Museum (Fourth Egyptian Room, Table-case B, No. 55585).

a very remarkable woman and that her influence over her husband was very great. Her name appears in the inscriptions side by side with that of her husband, a fact which proves that he acknowledged her authority as co-ruler with himself; and she assisted at public functions and in acts of ceremonial worship in a manner unknown to queens in Egypt before her time. Her power inside the palace and in the country generally was very great, and there is evidence that the king's orders, both private and public, were only issued after she had sanctioned them. In the Sûdân the king was worshipped as a god, and as the son and equal and counterpart of Åmen-Rā, and in the temple which Åmenḥetep built for her at Saddênga, some twenty or thirty miles south of Kôshah, Ti was worshipped as a goddess. When Åmenḥetep married her, or perhaps when he became king, he caused a number of unusually large steatite scarabs to be made, with his names and titles and those of Ti cut side by side on their bases.[1] On another group of large scarabs he caused his own names and titles, and the names of Ti and her father Iuåu and mother Thuåu, to be cut, and these are followed by the statement, "[She is] the wife of the victorious king whose territory in the South reaches to Karei (*i.e.*, Napata, at the foot of the Fourth Cataract) and in the North to Naharn" (*i.e.* the country of the head waters of the Euphrates).[2] Perhaps this is another way of saying the great and mighty king Åmenḥetep was proud to marry the daughter of parents of humble birth and to give her a position equal to his own. And it is possible, as Maspero suggested long ago, that some romantic episode

[1] For an example see No. 4094 in the British Museum (Table Case B. Fourth Egyptian Room).
[2] See Nos. 4096 and 16988.

is here referred to, similar to that in the old story where the king marries a shepherdess for love. What Ti's religious views were, or what gods she worshipped, we have no means of knowing, but the inscription which is found repeated on several large steatite scarabs suggests that she favoured the cult of Åten, and that in the later years of her life she was a zealous and devoted follower of that god. To please her Åmenḥetep caused a great lake to be made on her estate called Tchārukha  in Western Thebes. This lake was about 1⅛ mile (3,700 cubits) long and more than ⅝th of a mile (700 cubits) wide, and its modern representative is probably Birkat Habû. On the sixteenth day of the third month of the season Akhet (October), in the 11th year of his reign, His Majesty sailed over the lake in the barge called ÅTHEN-TEḤEN , *i.e.* "Åten sparkles." And in following years this day was celebrated as a festival. Both lake and barge were made to give the Queen pleasure, and the fact that the name of Åten formed part of the name of the latter, instead of Åmen, has been taken to show that both the King and Queen wished to pay honour to this solar god. In fact, it was definitely stated by Maspero that this water procession of the King marked the inauguration of the cult of Åten at Thebes, and he is probably correct.

Åmenḥetep's children by Ti consisted of four daughters and one son ; his daughters were called Ast, Henttaneb, Satåmen and Baktenåten, and her son was Åmenḥetep IV, the famous Åakhunåten. Ti lived in Western Thebes during her husband's lifetime, and she continued to do so after his death. She visited Tall al-'Amârnah from time to time, and was present there in the twelfth year of her son's reign. What appears to be an excellent portrait of her is reproduced on Plate XXXIII of Mr. Davis's book on her tomb.

But his respect for Ti and the honour in which he held her did not prevent Åmenḥetep from marrying other wives, and we know from the Tall al-'Amârnah tablets that he married a sister and a daughter of Tushratta, the King of Mitanni. His marriage with Gilukhipa, the daughter of Shutarna and sister of Tushratta, took place in the tenth year of his reign. And he commemorated the event by making a group of large scarabs inscribed on their bases with the statement that in the tenth year of his reign Gilukhipa , the daughter of Shutarna, prince of Neherna, arrived in Egypt with her ladies and escort of 317 persons.[1] Exactly when Åmenḥetep married Tushratta's daughter Tatumkhipa is not known, but that he received many gifts with her from her father is certain, for a tablet at Berlin (No. 296) contains a long list of her wedding gifts from her father. In marrying princesses of Mitanni Åmenḥetep followed the example of his father, Thothmes IV, whose wife, whom the Egyptians called Mutemuåa, was a native of that country. It follows as a matter of course that the influence of these foreign princesses on the King must have been very considerable at the Theban Court, and they and the high officials and ladies who came to Egypt with them would undoubtedly prefer the cult of their native gods to that of Åmen of Thebes. Ti's son, Åmenḥetep IV, and his sisters would soon learn their religious views, and the prince's hatred of Åmen and of his arrogant priesthood probably dates from the time when he came in contact with the princesses of Mitanni, and learned to know Mithras, Indra, Varuna and

[1] See No. 49707 in the British Museum.

other Aryan gods, whose cults in many respects resembled those of Horus, Rā, Tem and other Egyptian solar gods.

During the early years of his reign Ȧmenḥetep spent a great deal of his time in hunting, and to commemorate his exploits in the desert he caused two groups of large scarabs to be made. On the bases of these were cut details of his hunts and the numbers of the beasts he slew. One group of them, the "Hunt Scarabs," tells us that a message came to him saying that a herd of wild cattle had been sighted in Lower Egypt. Without delay he set off in a boat, and having sailed all night arrived in the morning near the place where they were. All the people turned out and made an enclosure with stakes and ropes, and then, in true African fashion, surrounded the herd and with cries and shouts drove the terrified beasts into it. On the occasion which the scarabs commemorate 170 wild cattle were forced into the enclosure, and then the King in his chariot drove in among them and killed 56 of them. A few days later he slew 20 more. This *battue* took place in the second year of Ȧmenḥetep's reign.[1]

The other group of "Hunt Scarabs" was made in the tenth year of his reign, and after enumerating the names and titles of Ȧmenḥetep and his wife Ti, the inscription states that from the first to the tenth year of his reign he shot with his own hand 102 fierce lions.[2] No other King of Egypt used the scarab as a vehicle for advertising his personal exploits and private affairs. That Ȧmenḥetep had some reason for so doing seems clear, but unless it was to secularize the sacred symbol of Kheperȧ, or to cast

[1] For a fine example of this group of scarabs, see No. 55585 in the British Museum.

[2] Fine examples in the British Museum are Nos. 4095, 12520, 24169 and 29438.

good-natured ridicule on some phase of native Egyptian belief which he thought lightly of, this use of the scarab seems inexplicable.

The reign of Åmenḥetep III stands alone in Egyptian History. When he ascended the throne he found himself absolute lord of Syria, Phœnicia, Egypt and the Egyptian Sûdân as far south as Napata. His great ancestor Thothmes III had conquered the world, as known to the Egyptians, for him. Save in the " war " which he waged in Nubia in the fifth year of his reign he never needed to strike a blow to keep what Thothmes III had won. And this " war " was relatively an unimportant affair. It was provoked by the revolt of a few tribes who lived near the foot of the Second Cataract, and according to the evidence of the sandstone stele, which was set up by Åmenḥetep to commemorate his victory, he only took 740 prisoners and killed 312 rebels.[1] In the Sûdân he made a royal progress through the country, and the princes and nobles not only acclaimed him as their over-lord but worshipped him as their god. And year by year, under the direction of the Egyptian Viceroy of Kash, they dispatched to him in Thebes untold quantities of gold, precious stones, valuable woods, skins of beasts, and slaves. When he visited Phœnicia, Syria, and the countries round about he was welcomed and acknowledged by the shêkhs and their tribes as their king, and they paid their tribute unhesitatingly. The great independent chiefs of Babylonia, Assyria, and Mitanni vied with each other in seeking his friendship, and probably the happiest times of his pleasure-

[1] The stele was made by Merimes, Viceroy of the Northern Sûdân, and set up by him at Samnah, some 30 miles south of Wâdî Ḥalfah. It is now in the British Museum. (Northern Egyptian Gallery, No. 411, Bay 6.) An illustration of it will be found in the *Guide*, p. 115.

loving life were the periods which he spent among his Mesopotamian friends and allies. His joy in hunting the lion in the desert south of Sinjâr and in the thickets by the river Khâbûr can be easily imagined, and his love for the chase would gain him many friends among the shêkhs of Mesopotamia. His visits to Western Asia stimulated trade, for caravans could travel to and from Egypt without let or hindrance, and in those days merchants and traders from the islands and coasts of the Mediterranean flocked to Egypt, where gold was as dust for abundance.

Åmenḥetep devoted a large portion of the wealth which he had inherited, and the revenues which he received annually from tributary peoples, to enlarging and beautifying the temples of Thebes. He had large ideas, and loved great and splendid effects, and he spared neither labour nor expense in creating them. He employed the greatest architects and engineers and the best workmen, and he gave them a "free hand," much as Ḥatshepsut did to her architect Senmut. On the east bank he made great additions to the temple of Karnak, and built an avenue from the river to the temple, and set up obelisks and statues of himself. He completed the temple of Mut and made a sacred lake on which religious processions in boats might take place. He joined the temples of Karnak and Luxor by an avenue of kriosphinxes, each holding a figure of himself between the paws, and at Luxor he built the famous colonnade, which is to this day one of the finest objects of its kind in Egypt. On the west bank he built a magnificent funerary temple, and before its pylon he set up a pair of obelisks and the two colossal statues of himself which are now known as the "Colossi of Memnon." A road led from the river to the temple, and each side of it was lined with stone figures of jackals. He also built on the Island of Elephantine a temple in honour of Khnemu, the great god of the First Cataract, and, as already said, he rebuilt and added largely to the temple which had been founded by Thothmes III at Ṣulb. All these temples were provided with metal-plated doors, parts of which seem to have been decorated with rich inlays, and colour was used freely in the scheme of decoration. The means at the king's disposal enabled him to employ unlimited labour, and most of his subjects must have gained their livelihood by working for Åmen and the king. Under such patrons as these the Arts and Crafts flourished, and artificers in stone, wood, brass, and faïence produced works the like of which had never before been seen in Egypt. Throughout his reign Åmenḥetep corresponded with his friends in Babylonia, Mitanni, and Syria, and the arrival and departure of the royal envoys gave opportunity for dispensing lavish hospitality, and for the display of wealth and all that it produces. The receptions in his beautifully decorated palace on the west bank of the river must have been splendid functions, such as the Oriental loves. The king spent his wealth royally; and in many ways, probably as a result of the Mitannian blood which flowed in his veins, his character was more that of a rich, luxury-loving, easy-going and benevolently despotic Mesopotamian Shêkh than that of a king of Egypt. Very aptly has Hall styled him "Åmenḥetep the Magnificent." He died after a reign of about thirty-six years, and was buried in his tomb in the Western Valley at Thebes. On the walls of the chambers there are scenes representing the king worshipping the gods of the Underworld, and on the ceiling are some very interesting astronomical paintings.

The tomb was unfinished when the king was buried in it. It was pillaged by the professional robbers of tombs, and the Government of the day removed his mummy to the tomb of Åmenḥetep II, where it was found by Loret in 1899. Thus whatever views Åmenḥetep III may have held about Åten, he was buried in Western Thebes, with all the pomp and ceremony befitting an orthodox Pharaoh.

DEVELOPMENT OF THE CULT OF ÅTEN UNDER ÅMENḤETEP IV.

Åmenḥetep III was succeeded by his son by his beloved wife Ti, who came to the throne under the name of Åmenḥetep IV. He reigned about seventeen years, and died probably before he was thirty. The accuracy of the latter part of this statement depends upon the evidence derived from the mummy of a young man which was found in the Tomb of Queen Ti, and is generally believed to be that of Åmenḥetep IV. It is thought that this mummy was taken from a royal tomb at Tall al-ʻAmârnah in mistake for that of Ti, and transported to Thebes, where it was buried as her mummy. Dr. Elliot Smith examined the skeleton, and decided that it was that of a man 25 or 26 years of age, "without excluding the possibility that he may have been several years older." His evidence[1] is very important, for he adds, "The cranium, however, exhibits in an unmistakable manner the distortion characteristic of a condition of hydrocephalus." So then if the skeleton be that of Åmenḥetep IV, the king suffered from water on the brain; and if he was 26 years old when he died he must have begun to reign at the age of nine or ten. But there is the possibility that he did not begin to reign until he was a few years older.

Even had his father lived, he was not the kind of man to teach his son to emulate the deeds of warrior Pharaohs like Thothmes III,

[1] See Davis, *The Tomb of Queen Tîyi*, London, 1910.

and there was no great official to instruct him in the arts of war, for the long peaceful reign of Ȧmenḥetep III made the Egyptians forget that the ease and luxury which they then enjoyed had been purchased by the arduous raids and wars of their forefathers. To all intents and purposes, Ti ruled Egypt for several years after her husband's death, and the boy-king did for a time at least what his mother told him. His wife, Nefertiti, who was his father's daughter probably by a Mesopotamian woman, was no doubt chosen for him by his mother, and it is quite clear from the wall-paintings at Tall al-'Amârnah that he was very much under their influence. His nurse's husband, Ȧi, was a priest of Ȧten, and during his early years he absorbed from this group of persons the fundamentals of the cult of Ȧten and much knowledge of the religious beliefs of the Mitannian ladies at the Egyptian Court. These sank into his mind and fructified, with the result that he began to abominate not only Ȧmen, the great god of Thebes, but all the old gods and goddesses of Egypt, with the exception of the solar gods of Heliopolis. In many respects these gods resembled the Aryan gods worshipped by his grandmother's people, especially Varuna, to whom, as to Rā, human sacrifices were sometimes offered, and to them his sympathy inclined. But besides this he saw, as no doubt many others saw, that the priests of Ȧmen were usurping royal prerogatives, and by their wealth and astuteness were becoming the dominant power in the land. Even at that time the revenues of Ȧmen could hardly be told, and the power of his priests pervaded the kingdom from Napata in the South to Syria in the North.

During the first five or six years of his reign Ȧmenḥetep IV, probably as the result of the

Plate VII.

Portion of a painted stone tablet with a portrait figure of Åmenḥetep IV in hollow relief. On him shine the rays of Åten which terminate in human hands.
British Museum, No. 24431.

Plate VIII.

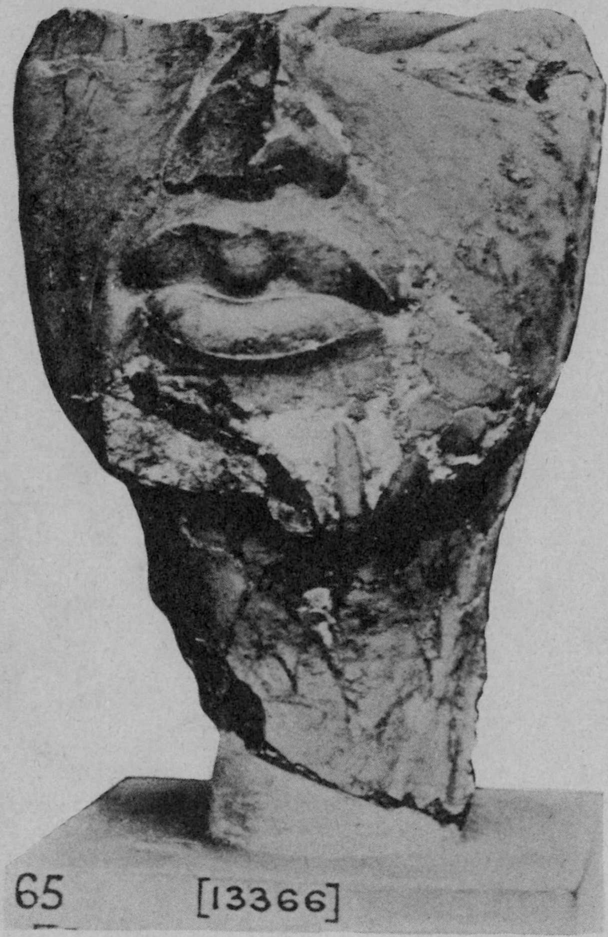

Portion of a head of a portrait figure of Åmenḥetep IV.
British Museum, No. 13366.

skilful guidance of his mother, made little or no change in the government of the country. But his actions in the sixth and following years of his reign prove that whilst he was still a mere boy he was studying religious problems with zeal, and with more than the usual amount of boyish understanding. He must have been precocious and clever, with a mind that worked swiftly; and he possessed a determined will and very definite religious convictions and a fearless nature. It is also clear that he did not lightly brook opposition, and that he believed sincerely in the truth and honesty of his motives and actions. But with all these gifts he lacked a practical knowledge of men and things. He never realized the true nature of the duties which as king he owed to his country and people, and he never understood the realities of life. He never learnt the kingcraft of the Pharaohs, and he failed to see that only a warrior could hold what warriors had won for him. Instead of associating himself with men of action, he sat at the feet of Ài the priest, and occupied his mind with religious speculations; and so, helped by his adoring mother and kinswomen, he gradually became the courageous fanatic that the tombs and monuments of Egypt show him to have been. His physical constitution and the circumstances of his surroundings made him what he was. In recent years he has been described by such names as "great idealist," "great reformer," the "world's first revolutionist," the "first *individual* in human history," etc. But, in view of the known facts of history, and Dr. Elliot Smith's remarks quoted above on the distortion of the skull of Àmenḥetep IV, we are fully justified in wondering with Dr. Hall if the king "was not really half insane."[1] None but a man half insane

[1] *Ancient History of the Near East*, p. 298.

would have been so blind to facts as to attempt to overthrow Åmen and his worship, round which the whole of the social life of the country centred. He

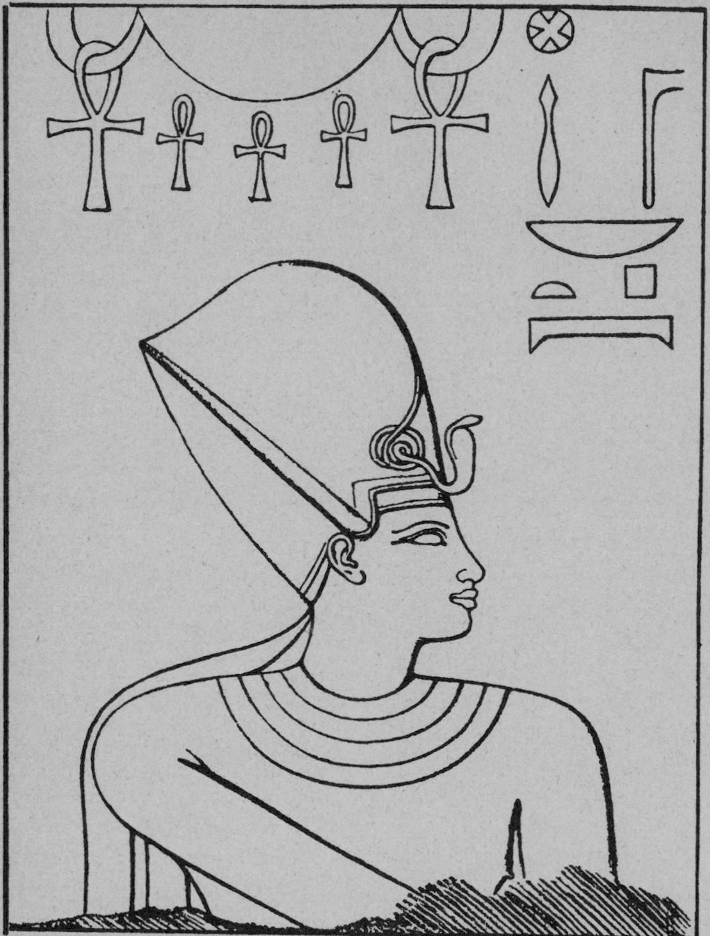

Åten, the great god, lord of heaven, from whom proceeds "life" ☥☥☥; beneath is Åmenḥetep IV who is here represented conventionally as a Pharaoh.

suffered from religious madness at least, and spiritual arrogance and self-sufficiency made him oblivious to everything except his own feelings and emotions.

Once having made up his mind that Åmen and all the other "gods" of Egypt must be swept away, Åmenḥetep IV determined to undertake this work without delay. After years of thought he had come to the conclusion that only the solar gods, Tem, Rā and Horus of the Two Horizons were worthy of veneration, and that some form of their worship must take the place of that of Åmen. The form of the Sun-god which he chose for worship was ÅTEN, *i.e.*, the solar Disk, which was the abode of Tem and later of Rā of Heliopolis. But to him the Disk was not only the abode of the Sun-god, it was the god himself, who, by means of the heat and light which emanated from his own body, gave life to everything on the earth. To Åten Åmenḥetep ascribed the attributes of the old gods, Tem, Rā, Horus, Ptaḥ, and even of Åmen, and he proclaimed that Aten was "One" and "Alone." But this had also been proclaimed by all the priesthoods of the old gods, Tem, Kheperå, Khnem, Rā, and, later, of Åmen. The worshippers of every great god in Egypt had from time immemorial declared that their god was "One." "Oneness" was an attribute, it would seem, of everything that was worshipped in Egypt, just as it is in some parts of India. It is inconceivable that Åmenḥetep IV knew of the existence of other suns besides the sun he saw, and it was obvious that Åten, the solar disk, was one alone, and without counterpart or equal. Some light is thrown upon Åmenḥetep's views as to the nature of his god by the title which he gave him. This title is written within two cartouches and reads :—

> "The Living Horus of the two horizons, exalted in the Eastern Horizon in his name of Shu-who-is-in-the-Disk."

It is followed by the words, "ever-living, eternal, great living Disk, he who is in the Seṭ Festival,[1] lord of the Circle (*i.e.*, everything which the Disk shines on in every direction), lord of the Disk, lord of heaven, lord of the earth." Ȧmenḥetep IV worshipped Horus of the two horizons as the "Shu who was in the disk." If we are to regard "Shu" as an ordinary noun, we must translate it by "heat," or "heat and light," for the word has these meanings. In this case Ȧmenḥetep worshipped the solar heat, or the heat and light which were inherent in the Disk. Now, we know from the Pyramid Texts that Tem or Tem-Rā created a god and a goddess from the emanations or substance of his own body, and that they were called "Shu" and "Tefnut," the former being the heat radiated from the body of the god, and the latter the moisture. Shu and Tefnut created Geb (the earth) and Nut (the sky), and they in turn produced Osiris, the god of the river Nile, Set, the god of natural decay and death, and their shadowy counterparts, Isis and Nephthys. But, if we regard "Shu" as a proper name in the title of Ȧmenḥetep's god, we get the same result, and can only assume that the king deified the heat of the sun and worshipped it as the one, eternal, creative, fructifying and life-sustaining force. The old Heliopolitan tradition made Tem or Tem-Rā, or Kheperȧ, the creator of Ȧten the Disk, but this view Ȧmenḥetep IV rejected, and he asserted that the Disk was self-created and self-subsistent. The common symbol of the solar gods was a

[1] The object of this festival seems to have been to prolong the life of the king, who dressed himself as Osiris, and assumed the attributes of Osiris, and by means of the rites and ceremonies performed became absorbed into the god. In this way the king renewed his life and divinity.

disk encircled by a serpent, but when Åmenḥetep adopted the disk as the symbol of his god, he abolished the serpent and treated the disk in a new and original fashion. From the disk, the circumference of which is sometimes hung round with symbols of "life," ☥, he made a series of rays to descend, and at the end of each ray was

The frog-headed goddess Ḥeqit, one of the Eight Members of the Ogdoad of Thoth.

a hand, as if the ray was an arm, bestowing "life" on the earth. This symbol never became popular in the country, and the nation as a whole preferred to believe that the Sun-god travelled across the sky in two boats, the Sektet and the Åtet. The form of the old Heliopolitan cult of the Sun-god that was evolved by Åmenḥetep could never have appealed to the Egyptians, for it was too philosophical in character and was probably based upon esoteric doctrines that were of foreign origin. Ḥer and Suti, the two great overseers of the temples of Ȧmen at Thebes, were content to follow the example of their king Ȧmenḥetep III, and bow the knee to Ȧten and, like other officials, to sing a hymn in his praise. But they knew the tolerant character of their master's religious views, and that outwardly at least he was a loyal follower of Ȧmen, whose blood, according to the dogma of his priests, flowed in the king's veins. To Ȧmenḥetep III a god more or less made no difference, and he considered it quite natural that every priesthood should extol and magnify the power of its god. He was content to be a counterpart of Ȧmen, and to receive the official worship due to him as such. But with his son it was different. The heat of Ȧten gave him life and maintained it in him, and whilst that was in him Ȧten was in him. The life of Ȧten was his life, and his life was Ȧten's life, and therefore he was Ȧten; his spiritual arrogance made him believe that he was an incarnation of Ȧten, *i.e.*, that he was God—not a mere "god" or one of the "gods" of Egypt—and that his acts were divine. He felt therefore that he had no need to go to the temple of Ȧmen to receive the daily supply of the "fluid of life," which not only maintained the physical powers of kings, but gave them wisdom and understanding to rule their country. Still less would he allow the high priest of Ȧmen to act as his vicar. Finally he determined that Ȧmen and the gods must be done away and all the dogmas and doctrines of their priesthoods abolished, and that Ȧten must be proclaimed the One, self-created, self-subsisting, self-existing god, whose son and deputy he was.

Without, apparently, considering the probable

Plate IX.

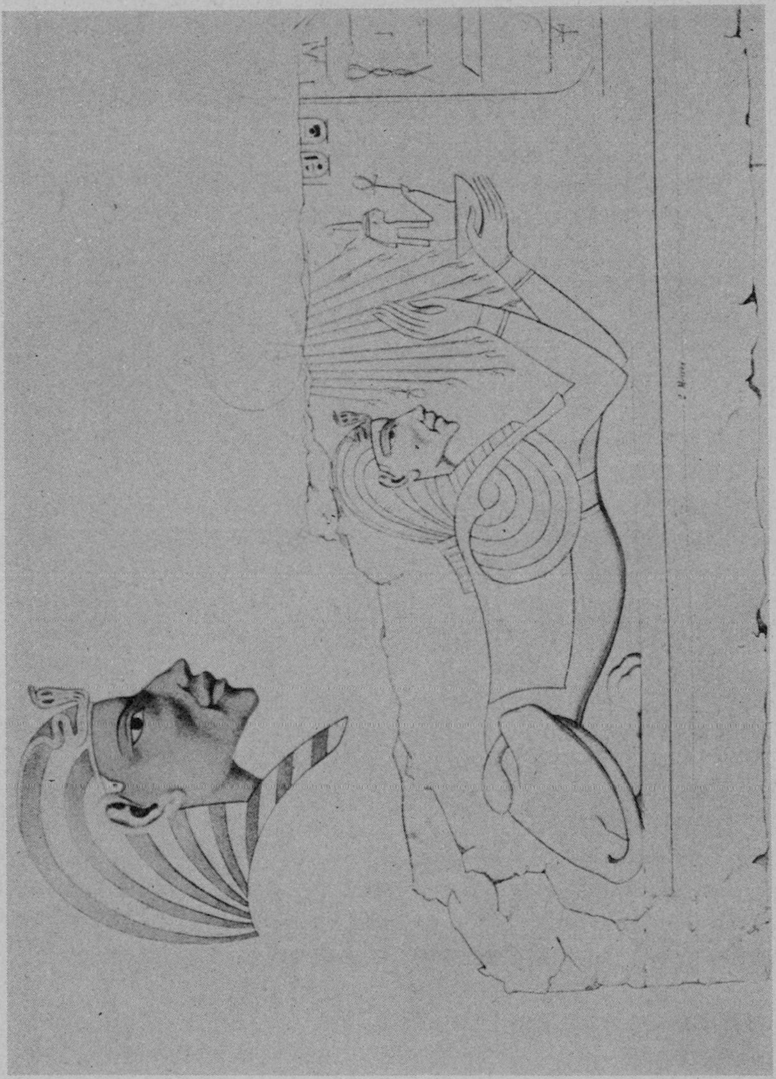

Sphinx, with the head of Åmenḥetep IV, making an offering of Maāt to Åten.

Plate X.

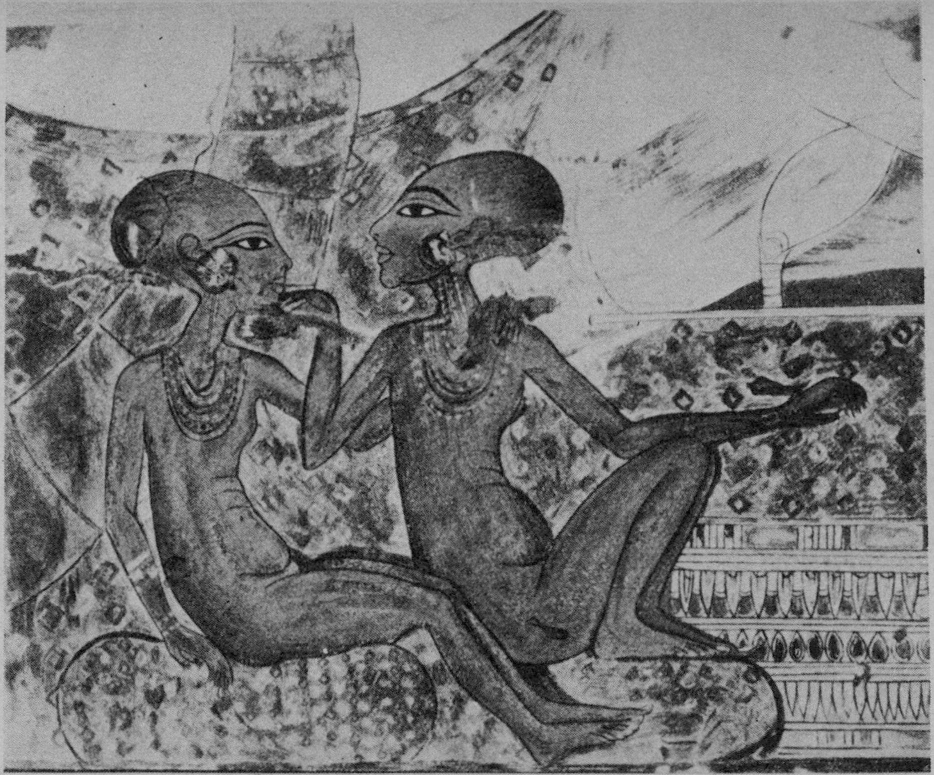

Two of the daughters of Åmenḥetep IV.
Reproduced by permission of the Committee of the Egypt Exploration Society.
From a bas-relief now in the Ashmolean Museum, Oxford.

effect of his decision when translated into action, he began to build the temple of Gem-Åten in Per-Åten, 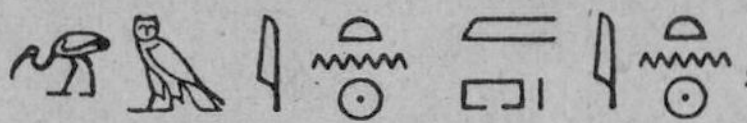, at Thebes. In it was a chamber or shrine, in which the *ben*, or *benben*, *i.e.*, the " Sun-stone," was placed, and in doing this he followed the example of the priests of Heliopolis. The site he selected for this temple was a piece of ground about half way between the Temple of Karnak and the Temple of Luxor. He decided that this temple should be the centre of the worship of Åten, which should henceforward be the one religion of his country. The effect of the king's action on the priests of Åmen and the people of Thebes can be easily imagined when we remember that with the downfall of Åmen their means of livelihood disappeared. But Åmenḥetep was the king, the blood of the Sun-god was in his veins, and Pharaoh was the master and owner of all Egypt, and of every person and thing in it. Priests and people were alike unable to resist his will, and, though they cursed Åten and his fanatical devotee, they could not prevent the confiscation of the revenues of Åmen and the abolition of his services. Not content with this, Åmenḥetep caused the name of Åmen to be obliterated on the monuments, and in some cases even his father's name, and the word for " gods "  was frequently cut out. Not only was there to be no Åmen, but there were to be no gods ; Åten was the only god that was to be worshipped.

The result of the promulgation of this decree can be easily imagined. Thebes became filled with the murmurings of all classes of the followers of Åmen, and when the temple of Åten was finished, and the worship of the new god was inaugurated, these murmurings were changed to threats and curses, and disputes between the Amenites and Atenites filled the city. What exactly happened is not known and never will be known, but the result of the confusion and uproar was that Åmenḥetep IV found residence in Thebes impossible, and he determined to leave it, and to remove the Court elsewhere. Whether he was driven to take this step through fear for the personal safety of himself and his family, or whether he wished still further to insult and injure Åmen and his priesthood, cannot be said, but the reason that induced him to abandon his capital city and to destroy its importance as such must have been very strong and urgent. Having decided to leave Thebes he sought for a site for his new capital, which he intended to make a City of God, and found it in the north, at a place which is about 160 miles to the south of Cairo and 50 miles to the north of Asyûṭ. At this point the hills on the east bank of the Nile enclose a sort of plain which is covered with fine yellow sand. The soil was virgin, and had never been defiled with temples or other buildings connected with the gods of Egypt whom Åmenḥetep IV hated, and the plain itself was eminently suitable for the site of a town, for its surface was unbroken by hills or reefs of limestone or sandstone. This plain is nearly three miles from the Nile in its widest part and is about five miles in length. The plain on the other side of the river, which extended from the Nile to the western hills, was very much larger than that on the east bank, and was also included by the king in the area of his new capital. He set up large stelæ on the borders of it to mark the limits of the territory of Åten, and had inscriptions cut upon them stating this fact.

We have already seen that Åmenḥetep IV had, whenever possible, caused the name of Åmen to be chiselled out from stelæ, statues, and other monuments, and even from his father's cartouches, whilst at the same time the name of Åmen formed part of his name as the son of Rā. It was easy to remedy this inconsistency, and he did so by changing his name from Åmenḥetep, which means "Åmen is content," to ÅAKHUNÅTEN, , a name which by analogy should mean something like "Åten is content." This meaning has already been suggested by more than one Egyptologist, but there is still a good deal to be said for keeping the old translation, "Spirit of Åten." I transcribe the new name of Åmenḥetep IV, Åakhunåten, not with any wish to add another to the many transliterations that have been proposed for it, but because it represents with considerable accuracy the hieroglyphs. The Pyramid Texts show that the phonetic value of  was  or . The first sign represents a short vowel, *ă*, *ĕ* or *ĭ*; the second *a*, like the Hebrew *aleph*, the third *kh*, and the fourth *u*; therefore the phonetic value of  in Pyramid times was *åakh*, or *åakhu*, but in later times the *å*  was probably dropped, and then the value of  would be *akh*, as Birch read it sixty years ago. If this were so, the name will be correctly transliterated by "Akhenåten." How the name was pronounced we do not know and never shall know, but there is no good ground for thinking that "Ikhnaton" or "Ikh-en-aton" represents the correct pronunciation. In passing we may note that *Åten* has nothing to do with the Semitic *'adhôn*, " lord."

At this time Åmenḥetep IV adopted two titles in connection with his new name, *i.e.*, " Ānkh-em-Maāt " and " Āa-em-āḥā-f," the former meaning, " Living in Truth " and the latter " great in his life period." What is meant exactly by

Thoth, lord of the writing of the god, *i.e.*, hieroglyphs. He was the mind of the primeval God, and translated into speech the will of this God.

Maāt, the goddess of truth, reality, law, both physical and spiritual, order, rectitude, uprightness, integrity, etc.

" living in truth " is not clear. *Maāt* means what is straight, true, real, law, both physical and moral, the truth, reality, etc. He can hardly have meant " living in or by the law," for he was a law to himself, but he may have meant that in Åtenism he had found the truth or the " real " thing, and that all else in religion was a phantom, a sham. Åten lived in *maāt*, or in truth and reality, and the king, having the essence of Åten in him, did the same. The exact meaning which Åmenḥetep IV attached to the other title, "great in his life-period," is also not clear. He, as was every Pharaoh who preceded him, was a "son of Rā," but he did not claim, as they did, to "live like Rā for ever," and only asserted that his life-period was great. Åmenḥetep IV called his new capital Åakhutåten, 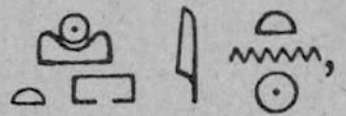, *i.e.*, "the Horizon of Åten," and he and his followers regarded it as the one place in which Åten was to be found. It was to them the visible symbol of the splendour and benevolence and love of the god, the sight of it rejoiced the hearts of all beholders, and its loveliness, they declared, was beyond compare. It was to them what Babylon was to the Babylonians, Jerusalem to the Hebrews, and Makkah to the Arabs; to live there and to behold the king, who was Åten's own son, bathed in the many-handed, life-giving rays of Åten, was to enjoy a foretaste of heaven, though none of the writers of the hymns to Åten deign to tell us what the heaven to which they refer so glibly was like. Having taken up his abode in this city, Åmenḥetep set to work to organize the cult of Åten, and to promulgate his doctrine, which, like all writers of moral and religious aphorisms, he called his "Teaching," , *Sbait*.

Having appointed himself High Priest, he, curiously enough, adopted the old title of the High Priest of Heliopolis and called himself "Ur-maa," , *i.e.*, the "Great Seer." But he did not at the same time institute the old

Åmenḥetep IV, accompanied by his queen and family, making offerings to Åten.

semi-magical rites and ceremonies which the holders of the title in Heliopolis performed. He did not hold the office very long, but transferred it to Merirā, one of his loyal followers.

When still a mere boy, probably before he ascended the throne and rejected his name of Åmenḥetep, he seems to have dreamed of building temples to Åten, and so when he took up his residence in his new city he at once set to work to build a sanctuary for that god. Among his devoted followers was one Bek, an architect and master builder, who claims to have been a pupil of the king, and who was undoubtedly a man of great skill and taste. Him the king sent to Sun, the Syene of the Greek writers, to obtain stone for the temple of Åten, and there is reason to think that, when the building was finished, its walls were most beautifully decorated with sculptures and pictures painted in bright colours. A second temple to Åten was built for the Queen-mother Ti, and a third for the princess Baktenåten, one of her daughters; and we should expect that one or more temples were built in the western half of the city across the Nile. With the revenues filched from Åmen Åakhunåten built several temples to Åten in the course of his reign. Thus he founded Per-gem-Åten in Nubia at a place in the Third Cataract; Gem-pa-Åten em Per-Åten at Thebes; Åakhutåten in Southern Ånu (Hermonthis); the House of Åten 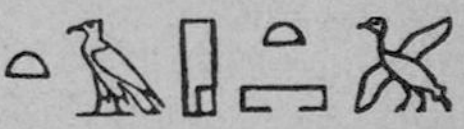 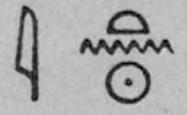 in Memphis; and Res-Rā-em-Ånu, . It will be noticed that no mention is made of Åten in the name of this last temple of Åten. He also built a temple to Åten in Syria, which is mentioned on one of the Tall

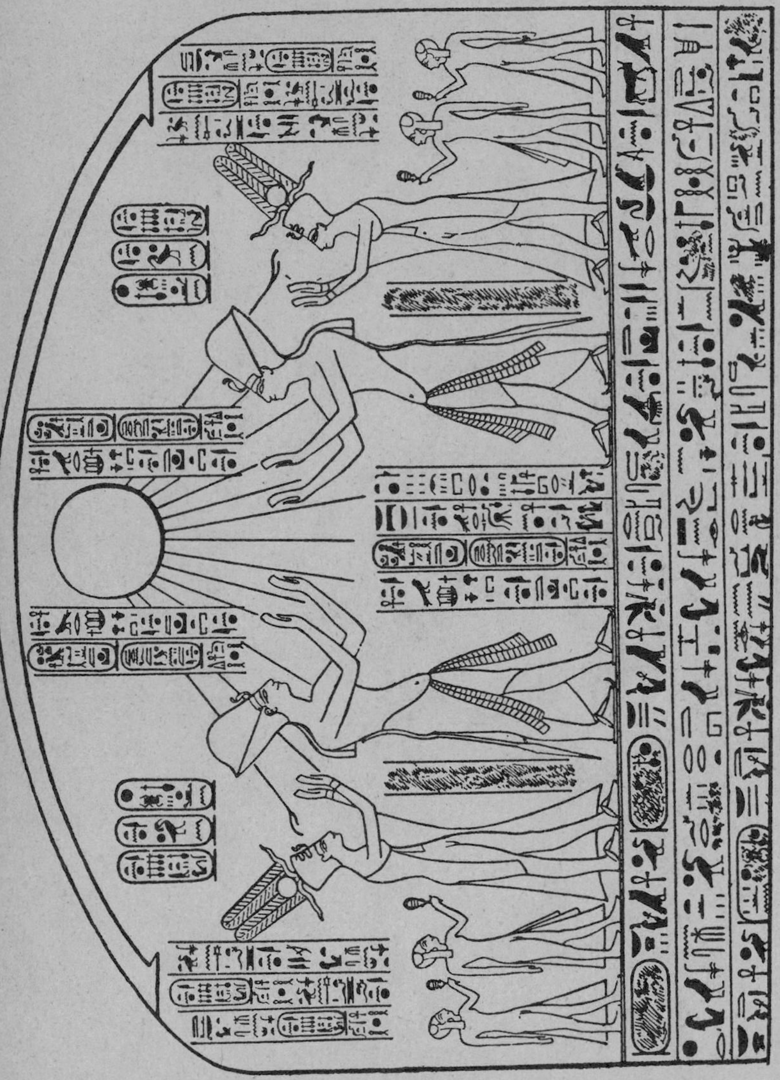

Amenhetep IV and his queen and family worshipping Āten.

al-'Amârnah tablets in the British Museum under the form Hi-na-tu-na 𒄭 𒈾 𒌅 𒈾.[1]

As the buildings increased in Åakhutåten and the cult of Åten developed, the king's love for his new city grew, and he devoted all his time to the worship of his god. Surrounded by his wife and family and their friends, and his obedient officials, who seem to have been handsomely rewarded for

Åmenḥetep IV and his Queen Nefertiti bestowing gold collars upon favourite courtiers. Between the king and queen is the princess Ånkh-s-en-pa-Åten, who married Tutānkhåmen, and behind the queen are two of her other daughters.

their devotion, the king had neither wish nor thought for the welfare of his kingdom, which he allowed to manage itself. His religion and his domestic happiness filled his life, and the inclinations and wishes of the ladies of his court had more weight with him than the counsels and advice of his ablest officials. We know nothing of the forms and ceremonies of the Åten worship, but hymns

[1] Babylonian Room, Table-Case F. No. 72 (29855).

and songs and choruses must have filled the temple daily. And the stele of Tutānkhåmen proves (see p. 9) that a considerable number of dancing men and acrobats were maintained by the king in connection with the service of Åten. Not only was the king no warrior, he was not even a lover of the chase. As he had no son to train in manly sports and to teach the arts of government and war, for his offspring consisted of seven daughters,[1] his officers must have wondered how long the state in which they were then living would last. The life in the City of Åten was no doubt pleasant enough for the Court and the official classes, for the king was generous to the officers of his government in the City, and, like the Pharaohs of old, he gave them when they died tombs in the hills in which to be buried. The names of many of these officers are well known, *e.g.*, Merirā I, Merirā II, Pa-neḥsi (the Negro), Ḥui, Åāhmes, Penthu, Māḥu, Åpi, Rāmes, Suti, Nefer-kheperu-ḥer-sekheper, Parennefer, Tutu, Åi, Māi, Ani, etc.[2]

[1] The names of the seven daughters of Åakhunåten were :—

1. Åten-merit, 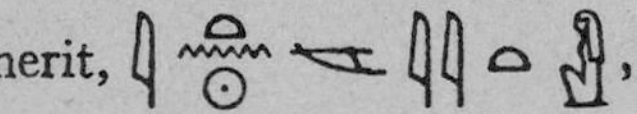, 2. Māket-Åten, 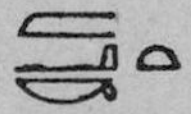 , 3. Ānkh-s-en-pa-Åten, , 4. Nefer-neferu-Åten the little, 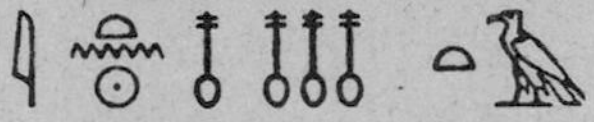 , 5. Nefer-neferu-Rā, 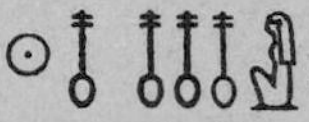, 6. Setep-en-Rā, , 7. Bakt-Åten, . The first daughter married her father's co-regent, Sākarā. The second died young and was buried in a tomb in the eastern hills. The third married Tutānkhåten (Åmen).

[2] The tombs of all these have been admirably published by Davies, *The Rock Tombs of El-Amarna*. Six vols. London, 1903–08.

Ȧmenhetep IV and his Queen Nefertiti and some of the daughters seated with the rays of Ȧten falling upon them. The queen wears the disk, horns, and plumes of Hathor and Isis. The abnormal development of the lower part of the body seems to be a characteristic of every member of the royal family.

The tombs of these men are different from all others of the same class in Egypt. The walls are decorated with pictures representing (1) the worship of Åten by the king and his mother; (2) the bestowal of gifts on officials by the king; (3) the houses, gardens and estates of the nobles; (4) domestic life, etc. The hieroglyphic texts on the walls of the tombs contain the names of those buried in them, the names of the offices which they held under the king, and fulsome adulation of the king, and of his goodness, generosity and knowledge. Then there are prayers for funerary offerings, and also Hymns to Åten. The long Hymn in the tomb of Åi is not by the king, as was commonly supposed; it is the best of all the texts of the kind in these tombs, and many extracts from it are found in the tombs of his fellow officials. A shorter Hymn occurs in some of the tombs, and of this it is probable that Åakhunåten was the author. We look in vain for the figures of the old gods of Egypt, Rā, Horus, Ptaḥ, Osiris, Isis, Anubis, and the cycles of the gods of the dead and of the Ṭuat (Underworld), and not a single ancient text, whether hymn, prayer, spell, incantation, litany, from the Book of the Dead in any of its Recensions is to be found there. To the Åtenites the tomb was a mere hiding place for the dead body, not a model of the Ṭuat, as their ancestors thought. Their royal leader rejected all the old funerary Liturgies like the "Book of Opening the Mouth," and the "Liturgy of funerary offerings," and he treated with silent contempt such works as the "Book of the Two Ways," the "Book of the Dweller in the Ṭuat," and the "Book of Gates." Thus it would appear that he rejected *en bloc* all funerary rites and ceremonies, and disapproved of all services of commemoration of the dead, which were so dear to the hearts of all Egyptians. The absence of figures of Osiris in the tombs of his officials and all mention of this god in the inscriptions found in them suggests that he disbelieved in the Last Judgment, and in the dogma of rewards for the righteous and punishments for evil doers. If this were so, the Field of Reeds, the Field of the Grasshoppers, the Field of Offerings in the

QEBHSENU-F, son of Osiris. | ṬUAMUTEF, son of Seker. | ḤEPI, son of Osiris. | MESTÅ.

The four grandsons of Horus the Aged. They were the gods of the four cardinal points, and later, as the sons of Osiris, protected the viscera of the dead.

Elysian Fields, and the Block of Slaughter with the headsman Shesmu, the five pits of the Ṭuat, and the burning of the wicked were all ridiculous fictions to him. Perhaps they were, but they were ineradicably fixed in the minds of his subjects, and he gave them nothing to put in the place of these fictions. The cult of Åten did not satisfy them, as history shows, for right or wrong, the

Egyptian, being of African origin, never understood or cared for philosophical abstractions. Another question arises: did the Ȧtenites mummify their dead? It is clear from the existence of the tombs in the hills about Ȧakhutȧten that important officials were buried; but what became of the bodies of the working class folk and the poor? Were they thrown to the jackals "in the bush"? All this suggests that the Ȧtenites adored and enjoyed the heat and light which their god poured upon them, and that they sang and danced and praised his beneficence, and lived wholly in the present. And they worshipped the triad of life, beauty and colour. They abolished the conventionality and rigidity in Egyptian painting and sculptures and introduced new colours into their designs and crafts, and, freed from the control of the priesthoods, artists and workmen produced extraordinarily beautiful results. The love of art went hand in hand with their religion and was an integral part of it. We may trace its influence in the funerary objects, even of those who believed in Osiris and were buried with the ancient rites and ceremonies especially in figures, vases, etc., made of pottery. Perhaps the brightly coloured vignettes, which are found in the great rolls of the Book of the Dead that were produced at this period, were painted by artists who copied the work of Ȧtenite masters.

Now whilst Ȧakhunȧten was organizing and developing the cult of Ȧten, and he and his Court and followers were passing their days and years in worshipping their god and in beautifying their houses, what was happening to the rest of Egypt? Tutānkhȧmen tells us that the revenues of the gods were diverted to the service of Ȧten, that the figures of the gods had disappeared from their thrones, that the temples were deserted, and that the Egyptians generally were living in a state of social chaos. For the first twelve years or so of Åakhunåten's reign the tribute of the Nubians was paid, for the Viceroy of Nubia had at hand means for making the tribes bring gold, wood, slaves, etc., to him. In the north of Egypt General

Åmenḥetep IV seated on his portable lion-throne beneath the rays of Åten; he holds in his hands the old Pharaonic symbols of sovereignty and dominion.

Ḥeremḥeb, the Commander-in-Chief, managed to maintain his lord's authority, but there is no doubt, as events showed when he became king of Egypt, that he was not a wholly sincere worshipper of Åten, and that his sympathies lay with the priesthoods of Ptaḥ of Memphis and

Rā of Heliopolis. The Memphites and the Heliopolitans must have resented bitterly the building of temples to Åten in their cities, and there can be little doubt that that astute soldier soon came to an understanding with them. Moreover, he knew better than his king what was happening in Syria, and how the Khabiru were threatening Phœnicia from the south, and how the Hittites were consolidating their position in Northern Syria, and increasing their power in all directions. He, and every one in Egypt who was watching the course of events, must have been convinced that no power which the king could employ could stop the spread of the revolt in Western Asia, and that the rule of the Egyptians there was practically at an end.

When the king as Åmenḥetep IV ascended the throne, all his father's friends in Babylonia, Assyria, Mitanni, the lands of the Kheta and Cyprus hastened to congratulate him, and all were anxious to gain and keep the friendship of the new king of Egypt. Burraburiyash, king of Karduniash, hoped that the new king and he would always exchange presents, and that the old friendship between his country and Egypt would be maintained. Ashuruballit sent him gifts and asked for 20 talents of gold in return. Tushratta, king of Mitanni, addressed him as " my son-in-law," sent greetings to Queen Ti, and spoke with pride of the old friendship between Mitanni and Egypt. He also wrote to Queen Ti, and again refers to the old friendship. But Åakhunåten did not respond in the manner they expected, and letters sent by them to him later show that the gifts which he sent were mean and poor. Clearly he lacked the open-handedness and generosity of his father Åmenḥetep III. As years went on, the governors of the towns and cities that were tributaries of Egypt wrote to the king protesting their devotion, fidelity and loyalty, many of them referring to favours received and asking for new ones. Very soon these protestations of loyalty were coupled with requests for

The rays of Åten giving "life" ☥ to Åmenḥetep IV whilst he is bestowing gifts on his favourite courtiers.

Egyptian soldiers to be sent to protect the king's possessions. Thus one Shuwardata writes: To the king, my lord, my gods and my Sun. Thus saith Shuwardata, the slave: Seven times and seven times did I fall down at the feet of the king my lord, both upon my belly and upon my back. Let the king, my lord, know that I am alone, and let the king, my lord, send troops in great multitudes, let the king, my lord, know this.[1]

The people of Tunip, who were vassals of Thothmes III, wrote and told the king that Aziru had plundered an Egyptian caravan, and that if help were not sent Tunip would fall as Ni had already done. Rib-Adda of Byblos writes: We have no food to eat and my fields yield no harvest because I cannot sow corn. All my villages are in the hands of the Khabiru. I am shut up like a bird in a cage, and there is none to deliver me. I have written to the king, but no one heeds. Why wilt thou not attend to the affairs of thy country? That "dog," Abd-Ashratum, and the Khabiri have taken Shigata and Ambi and Simyra. Send soldiers and an able officer. I beseech the king not to neglect this matter. Why is there no answer to my letters? Send chariots and I will try to hold out, else in two months' time Abd-Ashratum will be master of the whole country. Gebal (Byblos) will fall, and all the country as far as

[1] All these letters and reports are written in cuneiform upon clay tablets, of which over three hundred were found by a native woman at Tall al-'Amârnah in 1887-8. Summaries of the contents of those in the British Museum were published by Bezold and Budge in *Tell el-Amarna* Tablets, London, 1892, and by Bezold in *Oriental Diplomacy*, London, 1893. The texts of all the letters in London, Berlin, and Cairo were published, together with a German translation of them, by Winckler; another German translation was published by Knudtzon. The texts, with translations by Thureau-Dangin, of the six letters acquired by the Louvre in 1918, are published in *Revue d'Assyriologie*, Vol. XIX, Paris, 1921. Three of the letters are from Palestinian governors and two from Syrian chiefs; the third is by the King of Egypt and is addressed to Intaruda, governor of Aksaph.

Egypt will be in the hands of the Khabiri. We have no grain ; send grain. I have sent my possessions to Tyre, and also my sister's daughters for safety. I have sent my own son to thee, hearken to him. Do as thou wilt with me, but do not forsake thy city Gebal. In former times when Egypt neglected our city we paid no tribute ; do not thou neglect it. I have sold my sons and daughters for food and have nothing left. Thou sayest, "Defend thyself," but how can I do it ? When I sent my son to thee he was kept three months waiting for an audience. Though my kinsmen urge me to join the rebels, I will not do it.

Abi-Milki of Tyre writes : To the king, my lord, my gods, my Sun. Thus saith Abi-Milki, thy slave. Seven times and seven times do I fall down at the feet of the king my lord. I am the dust under the sandals of the king my lord. My lord is the sun that riseth over the earth day by day, according to the bidding of the Sun, his gracious Father. It is he in whose moist breath I live, and at whose setting I make my moan. He maketh all the lands to dwell in peace by the might of his hand ; he thundereth in the heavens like the Storm-god, so that the whole earth trembleth at his thunder. . . . Behold, now, I said to the Sun, the Father of the king my Lord, When shall I see the face of the king my Lord ? And now behold also I am guarding Tyre, the great city, for the king my lord until the king's mighty hand shall come forth unto me to give me water to drink and wood to warm myself withal. Moreover, Zimrida, the king of Sidon, sendeth word day by day unto the traitor Aziru, the son of Abd-Ashratum, concerning all that he hath heard from Egypt. Now behold, I have written unto my lord, for it is well that he should know this.

In a letter from Lapaya the writer says: If the king were to write to me for my wife I would not refuse to send her, and if he were to order me to stab myself with a bronzed dagger I would certainly do so. Among the writers of the Letters is a lady who reports the raiding of Ajalon and Sarha by the Khabiri. All the letters tell the same story of successful revolt on the part of the subjects of Egypt and the capture and plundering and burning of towns and villages by the Khabiri, and the robbery of caravans on all the trade routes. And whilst all this was going on the king of Egypt remained unmoved and only occupied himself with the cult of his god! The general testimony of the Tall al-'Amârnah Letters proves that he took no trouble to maintain the friendly relations that had existed between the kings of Babylonia and Mitanni and his father. He seems to have been glad enough to receive embassies and gifts from Mesopotamia, and to welcome flattering letters full of expressions of loyalty and devotion to himself, but the gifts which he sent back did not satisfy his correspondents. He sent little or no gold to be used in decorating temples in Mesopotamia and for making figures of gods, and some of the letters seem to afford instances of double-dealing on the part of the king of Egypt. At all events, he waged no wars in Mesopotamia, and when one city after another failed to send tribute he made no attempt to force them to do so. It is uncertain how much he really knew of what was happening in Western Asia, but when Tushratta and others sent him dispatches demanding compensation for attacks made upon their caravans, when passing through his territory, he must have realized that the power of Egypt in that country had greatly weakened. As the years went on he must have known that the Egyptians hated his god and loathed his rule, and such knowledge must have, more or less, affected the health of a man of his physique and character.

During the earlier years of his reign painters and sculptors gave him the conventional form of an Egyptian king, but later he is represented in an entirely different manner. He had naturally a long nose and chin and thick, protruding lips, and he was somewhat round-shouldered, and had a long slim body, and he must have had some deformity of knees and thighs. On the bas-reliefs and in the paintings all these physical characteristics are exaggerated, and the figures of the king are undignified caricatures.[1] But these must have been made with the king's knowledge and approval, and must be faithful representations of him as he appeared to those who made them. In other words, they are examples of the realism in art (which he so strongly inculcated in the sculptors and artists who claimed to be his pupils) applied to himself. History is silent as to the last years of his reign, but the facts now known suggest that, overwhelmed by troubles at home and abroad, and knowing that he had no son to succeed him, and that he had failed to make the cult of Åten the national religion, his proud and ardent spirit collapsed, and with it his health, and that he became a man of sorrow. Feeling his end to be near, he appointed as co-regent Sākarā tcheser-kheperu,[2] who had married his eldest

[1] Some interesting remarks by Dr. H. Asselbergs on the old and new style of bas-relief work in the reign of Åmenḥetep IV, with a photographic reproduction of a block published by Prisse in his *Monuments*, plate 10, No. 1, will be found in *Aegyptische Zeitschrift*, Band 58 (1923), p. 36 ff.

[2] His full titles are :—

daughter Merit-Åten, and died probably soon afterwards. He was buried in a rock-hewn tomb, which he had prepared in the hills five miles away on the eastern bank of the Nile instead of in the western hills, where all the kings of the XVIIIth dynasty were buried. Even in the matter of the position of his tomb he would not follow the custom of the country. This tomb was found in 1887–8 by native diggers, who cut out the cartouches of the king and sold them to travellers.

Under the section dealing with Åmenḥetep III reference has been made to the series of large steatite scarabs on which this king commemorated in writing noteworthy events in his life. Up to the present nothing has been found at Tall al-'Amârnah or in Egypt which would lead us to suppose that his son Åmenḥetep IV copied his example, but a very interesting scarab found at Sadênga in the Egyptian Sûdân[1] proves that he did, at least on one occasion. This scarab is now in the British Museum (No. 51084). On one side of the body of the scarab is the king's prenomen  and on the other is his nomen 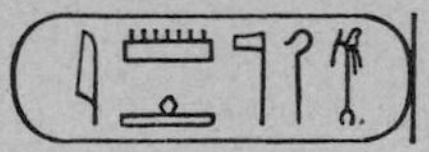. On the base, which is mutilated at the sides, are seven lines of text which read :—

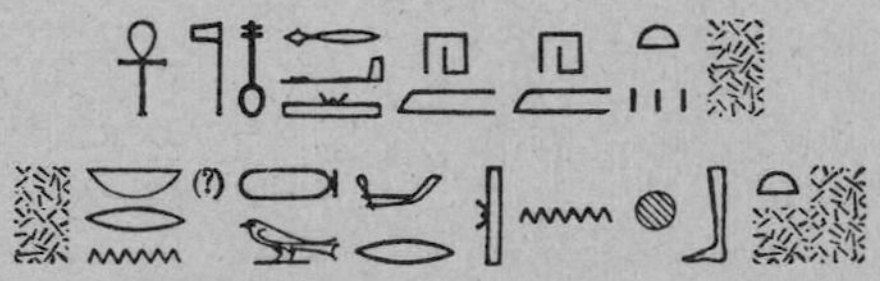

[1] It was first published by Hall, *Catalogue of Scarabs*, p. 302.

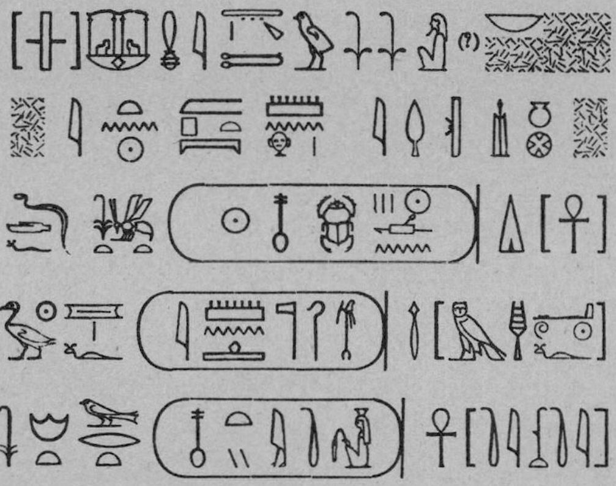

This inscription shows that the scarab was made for Åmenḥetep IV before he adopted his new name of Åakhunåten. The last three lines give names and titles of the king and his queen, and the first four contain an address or prayer concerning some god. The breaks at the beginnings and ends of the lines do not permit a connected translation to be made, but the general meaning of the inscription is as follows :—

"The king of the South and of the North, Nefer-kheperu-Rā-uā-en-Rā, giver of life, son of Rā, loving him, Åmenḥetep, God, Governor of Thebes, great in the duration of his life, [and] the great royal wife Nefertiti, living and young, say: Long live the Beautiful God, the great one of roarings (thunders?) . . . in the great and holy name of . . . Dweller in the Seṭ Festival like Ta-Thunen, the lord of . . . the Åten (Disk) in heaven, stablished of face, gracious (or pleasant) in Ånu (On)." This address or prayer seems to have been made to some Thunder-god, whose name was great and holy: the ordinary god of the thunder in Egypt was Āapep, who in this character is called "Hemhem-ti." The mention of Tathunen is interesting, for he was, of course, one of the "gods" whom Åmenḥetep IV at a later period of his life wished to abolish. Can this inscription represent an attempt to assimilate an indigenous Sûdânî Thunder-god with Åten? The writer of one of the Tall al-'Amârnah Letters quoted above (p. 101) speaks of the Thundering of Åmenḥetep IV, and says that when he thunders all the people quake with fear. From this it seems that some phase of Åten was associated in the minds of foreigners with the Thunder-god, but there is no evidence to show who that god was.

The facts known about the life and reign of Åakhunåten seem to me to prove that from first to last he was a religious fanatic, intolerant, arrogant and obstinate, but earnest and sincere in his seeking after God and in his attempts to make Åten the national god of Egypt. Modern writers describe him as a "reformer," but he reformed nothing. He tried to force the worship of "Horus of the Two Horizons in his name of Shu (*i.e.*, Heat) who is in the Åten" upon his people and failed. When he found that his subjects refused to accept his personal views about an old, perhaps the oldest, solar god, whose cult had been dead for centuries, he abandoned the capital of his great and warlike ancestors in disgust, and like a spoilt child, which no doubt he was, he withdrew to a new city of his own making. Like all such religious megalomaniacs, so long as he could satisfy his own peculiar aspirations and gratify his wishes, no matter at what cost, he was content. Usually the harm which such men do is limited in character and extent, but he, being a king, was able to inflict untold misery on his country during the seventeen years of his reign. He spent the revenues of his country on the cult of his god, and in satisfying his craving for beauty in shape and form, and for ecstatic religious emotion. Though lavish in the rewards in good gold and silver to all those who ministered to this craving, he was mean and niggardly when it came to spending money for the benefit of his country. The Tall al-'Amârnah Letters make this fact quite clear. The peoples of Western Asia might think and say that the King of Egypt had "turned Fakîr," but there was little asceticism in his life. His boast of "living in reality," or "living in truth," which suggests that he lived a perfectly natural and simple life, seeing things as they really were, on the face of it seems to be ludicrous. Åakhunåten had much in common with Al-Hâkim, the Fâtimid Khalîfah of Egypt (A.D. 996–1021). Each was the son of a wealthy, pleasure-loving, luxurious father, and each succeeded to the throne when he was a boy. Each had a strange face, each was moved to break with tradition and introduce new ideas, but the spirit in which each made changes was that of a mad reformer. Christians and Jews were to Al-Hâkim what the Åmenites were to Åakhunåten. Both king and Khalîfah were pious in an intolerant and arrogant fashion, and each was a builder of places for worship. Each thought that he was the incarnation of God, and each usurped the attributes of the Deity, and prescribed rules for worship. Each was a patron of the arts, but there is no evidence that the Pharaoh encouraged learned men to flock to his Court as did the Khalîfah. Al-Hâkim frequently had his enemies murdered, and in his fits of rage had people killed wholesale. Though we have no knowledge that such atrocities were committed at Åakhutåten, yet it would be rash to assume that persons who incurred the king's displeasure in a serious degree were not removed by the methods that have been well known at Oriental Courts from time immemorial.

Åakhunåten was succeeded by his co-regent Sākarā, whose reign was probably very short and unimportant. He was the son-in-law of the king and a devoted worshipper of Åten, whose cult he wished to make permanent. Nothing is known of his acts or whether deposition or death removed him from the throne. He was succeeded by Tutānkhåmen, whose reign has been already described. The short reign of Åi, who had married the nurse of Åmenḥetep IV, and was Master of the Horse, followed, and he was succeeded by Ḥer-em-ḥeb, a military officer who served in the north of Egypt during the reign of Åakhunåten. The restoration of the cult of Åmen begun by Tutānkhåmen was finally confirmed by him, and the triumph of Åmen was complete. The immediate result of this was the decline and fall of the cult of Åten, and the city "Horizon of Åten" lost all its importance and fell into decay. The artisan classes, finding no work, migrated to Thebes and other places where they could ply their crafts in the service of Åmen, and many of the Åtenites abandoned their god and transferred their worship to Åmen. It is probable that the temples and houses of the officials were plundered by the mob, who treated them in the way that the property of an overthrown religious faction has always been treated in the East. The forsaken city soon fell into ruins and was never rebuilt or again inhabited. A liberal estimate for the life of the city is 50 years.

The remains of Åakhutåten are marked to-day by the ruins and rock-hewn tombs which lie near the Arab villages of Ḥagg Ḳandîl and At-Tall, and are commonly known as "Tall al-'Amârnah." In 1887 this name was in common use among the Egyptians of Upper Egypt, and I asked Mustafa Agha, H.B.M.'s Vice-Consul at Luxor, to explain it. He said that the Bani 'Amrân Arabs settled at At-Tall (ordinarily pronounced At-Tell, or even At-Till), and that for many years the village was known as "Tall Bani 'Amrân." When most of the Bani 'Amrân left the place and returned to the desert, the village was called "Tall al-'Amârnah" (pronounced Tellel-'Amârnah). The site, which is a very large one, needs careful excavation from one end to the other, for only here can possibly be found material for the real history of Åmenḥetep IV and his reign. The discoveries already made there prove this, for over three hundred Letters and Despatches written in cuneiform from kings and governors in Western Asia were found on the site by a woman in 1887,[1] and she sold them to a neighbour for 10 piastres (2*s*.). As a result of the woman's discovery Petrie made excavations at Tall al-'Amârnah and succeeded in finding several small fragments and chips of lists of signs and words, etc., and some beautifully painted pavements.[2] The Deutsche Orient-Gesellschaft began to excavate there in 1913, and in the year following they discovered a number of very important objects, among which may be specially mentioned a cuneiform tablet and a marvellously beautiful head of Queen Nefertiti, which is now in the Museum at Berlin. This head is the finest example known of the painted sculpture work from Tall al-'Amârnah, and should have been

[1] This discovery has been attributed to Petrie by Mr. Garvin in the *Observer*, February 25, 1923. I have told the true story of the "find" in my *Nile and Tigris*, Vol. 1, p. 140 ff.

[2] He dug there from November, 1891, to the end of March, 1892. See his *Tell el Amarna*, London, 1894, 4to.

kept in Egypt and placed in the Egyptian Museum at Cairo. This oversight on the part of the officials of the Cairo Museum seems to require an explanation. Among the cuneiform fragments discovered by the German excavators at Tall al-'Amârnah in 1913 was one which was inscribed with a legend describing the expedition of Sargon of Akkad to Asia Minor. The original text of the legend of the " King of the Battle " is published by Schroeder in *Vorderasiatische Schriftdenkmäler*, xii, pp. 2–4, and it has been translated by Weidner under the title of *Der Zug Sargons von Akkad nach Kleinasien*.

In the winter of 1920–21 the Egypt Exploration Society sent out an expedition to Tall al-'Amârnah, under the direction of Prof. T. E. Peet, to carry on the work of excavation from the point where the Germans left it in 1914. During the course of the work a considerable number of very interesting objects were found, including a fragment of a cuneiform tablet, inscribed with a list of signs, and some fine examples of variegated glass vessels and pottery. The data he collected[1] answered a number of questions and settled some difficulties, and the Society determined to continue their excavation of the site. In 1922 Mr. Woolley succeeded Prof. Peet as Director of the Expedition, and continued the work as long as funds permitted. The discovery made by Lord Carnarvon and Mr. Howard Carter in December, 1922, has stirred up public interest in all that concerns the reigns of Tutānkhāmen and his predecessor Åmenḥetep IV, the notorious " Heretic King." It is more necessary now than ever that excavations should be carried on until

[1] See his preliminary Report in the *Journal of Egyptian Archæology*, Vol. VII (1921), p. 169 ff.

the ruins at Tall al-'Amârnah have been thoroughly cleared and examined. In order to do this the Egypt Exploration Society must be liberally supported, and everyone who is interested in the History and Religion of the ancient Egyptians should subscribe to this work. Like everything else, the cost of excavating sites has increased in recent years, and subscriptions to the Society have not increased in proportion to the expenses. The President of the Society is the Right Hon. General J. Grenfell Maxwell, G.C.B., who is himself an ardent collector of Egyptian antiquities, and the Hon. Secretary is Dr. H. R. Hall, Deputy Keeper of the Department of Egyptian and Assyrian Antiquities in the British Museum. The excavations and other operations of the Society are conducted with strict regard to efficient economy, and all the objects obtained from the excavations are distributed *gratis* among Museums.

Hymns to Åten.

The first Hymn (A) is put into the mouth of Åakhunåten, and is known as the "Shorter Hymn to Åten." Several copies of it have been found in the tombs at Tall al-'Amârnah. Texts of it have been published by Bouriant, Daressy, Piehl and others, but the most correct version is that copied from the tomb of Åpi and published by Mr. N. de G. Davies.[1] The second Hymn (B) is found in the tomb of Åi, and is known as the "Longer Hymn to Åten." The text was first published by Bouriant in *Mission Archéologique*, tom. I, p. 2, but badly, and he revised it in his *Monuments du Culte d'Atonou*, I., pl. xvi. A good

[1] For the published literature see his *Rock Tombs*, Vol. IV, p. 28.

text with a Latin translation was published by Breasted in his *De Hymnis in Solem sub rege Amenophide IV conceptis*, Berlin, 1894, and English versions of most of it were given by him in his *History of Egypt*, p. 315, and in other publications. Other versions and extracts have been published by Griffith, *World's Literature*, p. 5225; Wiedemann, *Religion*, pp. 40–42; Hall, *Ancient History*, p. 306; Erman, *Religion*, p. 64, etc. The best text yet published is that of Davies[1] and that, with a few trivial alterations, is reproduced in the following pages. In recent years this Hymn has been extolled as a marvellously beautiful religious composition, and parts of it have been compared with some of the Hebrew Psalms. In consequence it has been regarded as an expression of sublime human aspirations, and the outcome of a firm belief in a God who was a counterpart of the Yahweh of the Hebrews and identical with God Almighty. But if we examine the Hymn, line by line, and compare it with the Hymns to Rā, Åmen and other gods, we find that there is hardly an idea in it which is not borrowed from the older Egyptian religious books. Åten is called the eternal, almighty, self-produced, living, or self-subsisting, creator of heaven and earth and all that is in them, and "one god alone." His heat and light are the sources of all life, and only for these and the material benefits that they confer on man and beast is Åten praised in these hymns. There is nothing spiritual in them, nothing to appeal to man's higher nature. The language in which they are written is simple and clear, but there is nothing remarkable about the phraseology, unless the statements are dogmatic declarations like

[1] *Ibid.*, Vol. VI, pl. xxvii.

the articles of a creed. A very interesting characteristic of the hymns to Àten is the writer's insistence on the beauty and power of light, and it may be permitted to wonder if this is not due to Mitannian influence, and the penetration into Egypt of Aryan ideas concerning Mitra, Varuna, and Sûrya or Savitri, the Sun-god. Àten, or Horus of the Two Horizons, corresponds closely to Sûrya, the rising and setting sun, Rā to Savitri, the sun shining in full strength, "the golden-eyed, the golden-handed, and golden tongued." "As the Vivifier and Quickener, he raises his long arms of gold in the morning, rouses all beings from their slumber, infuses energy into them, and buries them in sleep in the evening."[1] Sûrya, the rising and setting sun, like Àten, was the great source of light and heat, and therefore Lord of life itself. He is the Dyaus Pitar, the "Heaven-Father." Àten, like Sûrya, was the "fountain of living Light,"[2] with the all-seeing eye, whose beams revealed his presence, and "gleaming like brilliant flames"[3] went to nation after nation. Àten was not only the light of the sun, which seems to give new life to man and to all creation, but the giver of light and all life in general. The bringer of light and life to-day, he is the same who brought light and life on the first of days, therefore Àten is eternal. Light begins the day, so it was the beginning of creation; therefore Àten is the creator, neither made with hands nor begotten, and is the Governor of the world. The earth was fertilized by Àten, therefore he is the Father-Mother of all creatures. His eye saw everything and knew everything. The hymns to Àten suggest that

[1] Wilkins, *Hindu Mythology*, p. 33.
[2] See Martin, *Gods of India*, p. 35.
[3] Monier-Williams, *Indian Wisdom*, p. 19.

Åmenḥetep IV and his followers conceived an image of him in their minds and worshipped him inwardly. But the abstract conception of thinking was wholly inconceivable to the average Egyptian, who only understood things in a concrete form. It was probably some conception of this kind that made the cult of Åten so unpopular with the Egyptians, and caused its downfall. Åten, like Varuna, possessed a mysterious presence, a mysterious power, and a mysterious knowledge. He made the sun to shine, the winds were his breath, he made the sea, and caused the rivers to flow. He was omniscient, and though he lived remote in the heavens he was everywhere present on earth. And a passage in the Rig-Veda would form an admirable description of him.

> Light-giving Varuna! Thy piercing glance doth scan
> In quick succession all this stirring active world.
> And penetrateth, too, the broad ethereal space,
> Measuring our days and nights and spying out all creatures.[1]

But Varuna possessed one attribute, which, so far as we know, was wanting in Åten; he spied out sin and judged the sinner. The early Aryan prayed to him, saying, "Be gracious, O Mighty God, be gracious. I have sinned through want of power; be gracious. What great sin is it, Varuna, for which thou seekest in thy worshipper and friend? Tell me, O unassailable and self-dependent god; and, freed from sin, I shall speedily come to thee for adoration."[2]

[1] Monier-Williams' translation.
[2] Rig-Veda, VII, 86, 3–6.

And Varuna was a constant witness of men's truth and falsehood. The early Aryan also prayed to Sûrya, and addressed to him the Gâyatrî, a formula which is the mother of the Vedas and of the Brâhmans. He said to the god, " May we attain the excellent glory of the divine Vivifier : so may he enlighten or stimulate our understanding." The words secured salvation for a man.[1] No consciousness of sin is expressed in any Ȧten text now known, and the Hymns to Ȧten contain no petition for spiritual enlightenment, understanding or wisdom. For what then did the follower of Ȧten pray ? An answer to this question is given in the Teaching of Ȧmenemȧpt, the son of Kanekht, who says :—

" Make the prayer which is due from thee to the
  Ȧten, when he is rising,
Say, Grant to me, I beseech, strength [and]
  health.
He will give thy provision for the life.
And thou shalt be safe from that which would
  terrify [thee]."[2]

[1] Martin, *The Gods of India*, p. 39.

[2] *Hieratic Papyri in the British Museum*, ed. Budge, 2nd Series, London, 1923, pl. 5.

A.—A HYMN TO ȦTEN BY THE KING.[1]

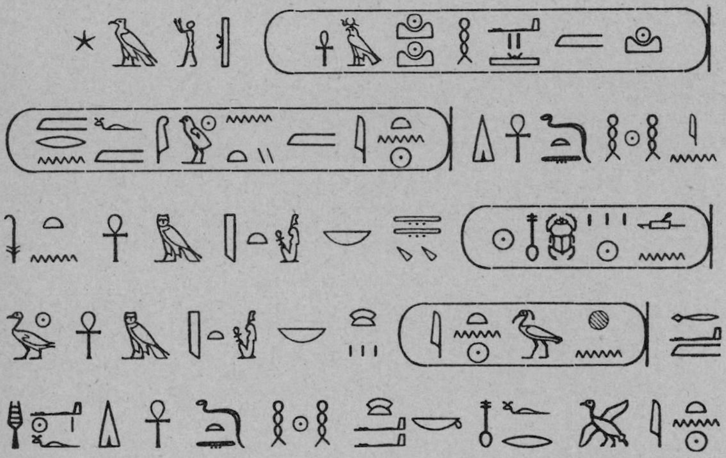

A Hymn of Praise to the living Horus of the Two Horizons, who rejoiceth in the horizon in his name of "Shu, who is in the Ȧten" (*i.e.*, Disk), the giver of life for ever and ever, by the King who liveth in truth, the Lord of the Two Lands, Nefer-kheperu-Rā Uā-en-Rā, Son of Rā, who liveth in Truth, Lord of the Crowns, Aakhunȧten, great in the duration of his life, giver of life for ever and ever.

[1] See N. de G. Davies, *The Rock Tombs of El Amarna*, Vol. IV, pl. xxxii, xxxiii. The text is from the Tomb of Ȧpi at Tall al-'Amârnah, with an addition from the tomb of Tutu.

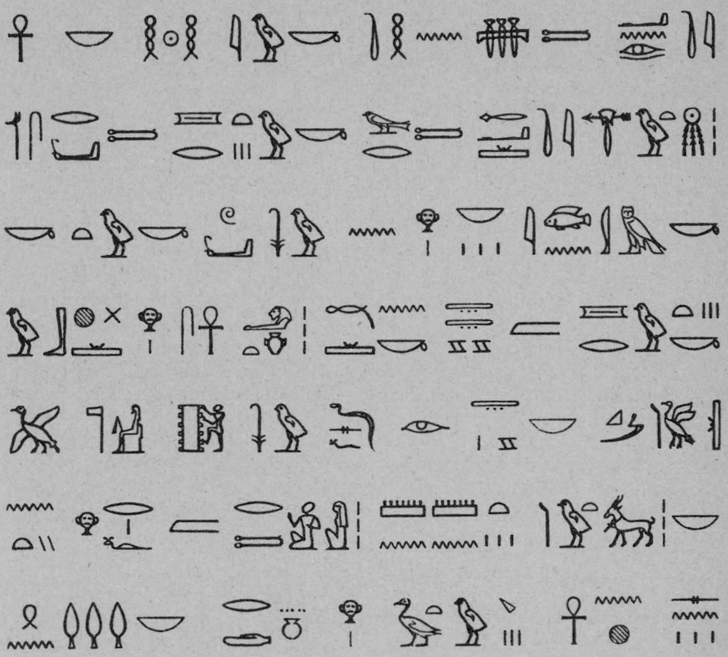

[He saith] :—

Thou risest gloriously, O thou Living Åten, Lord of Eternity! Thou art sparkling (or coruscating), beautiful, [and] mighty. Thy love is mighty and great . . . thy light, of diverse colours, leadeth captive (or, bewitcheth) all faces. Thy skin shineth brightly to make all hearts to live. Thou fillest the Two Lands with thy love, O thou god, who did[st] build [thy]self. Maker of every land, Creator of whatsoever there is upon it, [viz.] men and women, cattle, beasts of every kind, and trees of every kind that grow on the land.

They live when thou shinest upon them. Thou art the mother [and] father of what thou hast made; their eyes, when thou risest, turn their gaze upon thee. Thy rays at dawn light up the whole earth. Every heart beateth high at the sight of thee, [for] thou risest as their Lord.

Thou settest in the western horizon of heaven, they lie down in the same way as those who are dead. Their heads are wrapped up in cloth, their nostrils are blocked, until thy rising taketh place at dawn in the eastern horizon of heaven. Their hands then are lifted up in adoration of thy

Ka (or person); thou vivifiest hearts with thy beauties (or, beneficent acts), which are life. Thou sendest forth thy beams, [and] every land is in festival. Singing men, singing women, [and] chorus men make joyful noises in the Hall of the House of the Benben Obelisk, [and] in every temple in [the city of] Åakhut-Åten, the Seat of Truth, wherewith thy heart is satisfied. Within it are dedicated offerings of rich food (?).

Thy son is sanctified (or, ceremonially pure) to perform the things which thou willest, O thou Åten, when he showeth himself in the appointed processions.

Every creature that thou hast made skippeth towards thee, thy honoured son [rejoiceth], his heart is glad, O thou Living Åten, who [appearest] in heaven every day. He hath brought forth his honoured son, UĀ-EN-RĀ, like his own form, never ceasing so to do. The son of Rā supporteth his beauties (or beneficent acts).

NEFER-KHEPERU-RĀ UĀ-EN-RĀ [saith] :—

I am thy son, satisfying thee, exalting thy name. Thy strength [and] thy power are established in my heart. Thou art the Living Disk, eternity is thine emanation (or, attribute). Thou hast made the heavens to be remote so that thou

mightest shine therein and gaze upon everything that thou hast made. Thou thyself art Alone, but there are millions of [powers of] life in thee to make them (*i.e.*, thy creatures) live. Breath of life is it to [their] nostrils to see thy beams. Buds burst into flower (?), [and] the plants which grow on the waste lands send up shoots at thy rising; they drink themselves drunk before thy face. All the beasts frisk about on their feet; all the feathered fowl rise up from their nests and flap their wings with joy, and circle round in praise of the Living Åten. . . .

[1] The passage in brackets is added from another copy of the Hymn, viz., that of Tutu.

B.—HYMN TO ÀTEN[1]

BY

ÀI, OVERSEER OF THE HORSE OF ÀAKHUNÀTEN.

1.

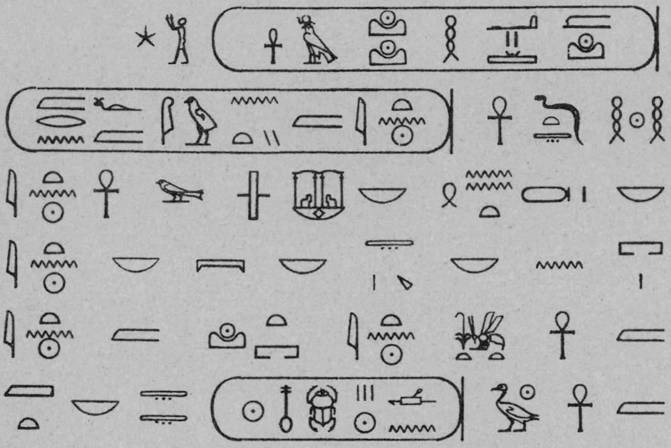

1. A Hymn of praise of Ḥer-àakhuti, the living one, exalted in the Eastern Horizon in his name of Shu who is in the Àten, who liveth for ever and ever, the living and great Àten, he who is in the Seṭ-Festival, the lord of the Circle, the Lord of the Disk, the Lord of heaven, the Lord of earth, the lord of the House of the Àten in Àakhut-Àten, [of] the King of the South and the North, who liveth in Truth, lord of the Two Lands (*i.e.*, Egypt), NEFER-KHEPERU-RĀ UĀ-EN-RĀ, the son of Rā,

[1] See N. de G. Davies, *op. cit.*, Vol. VI, pl. xxvii.

2.

who liveth in Truth, Lord of Crowns, ÅAKHUN-ÅTEN, great in the period of his life, [and of] the great royal woman (or wife) whom he loveth, Lady of the Two Lands, NEFER-NEFERU-ÅTEN NEFERTITI, who liveth in health and youth for ever and ever.

2. He (*i.e.*, Åi, a Fan-bearer and the Master of the King's Horse) saith :—

Thy rising [is] beautiful in the horizon of heaven, O Åten, ordainer of life. Thou dost shoot up in the horizon of the East, thou fillest every land with thy beneficence. Thou art beautiful and great and sparkling, and exalted above every land. Thy arrows

3.

(*i.e.*, rays) envelop (*i.e.*, penetrate) everywhere all the lands which thou hast made.

3. Thou art as Rā. Thou bringest [them] according to their number, thou subduest them for thy beloved son. Thou thyself art afar off, but thy beams are upon the earth; thou art in their faces, they [admire] thy goings.

Thou settest in the horizon of the west, the earth is in darkness, in the form of death. Men lie down in a booth wrapped up in cloths, one eye cannot see its fellow.

If all their possessions, which are under their heads, be carried away they perceive it not.

4. Every lion emergeth from his lair, all the creeping things bite, darkness [is] a warm retreat (?). The land is in silence. He who made them hath set in his horizon.

The earth becometh light, thou shootest up in the horizon, shining in the Àten in the day, thou scatterest the darkness. Thou sendest out thine arrows (*i.e.*, rays),

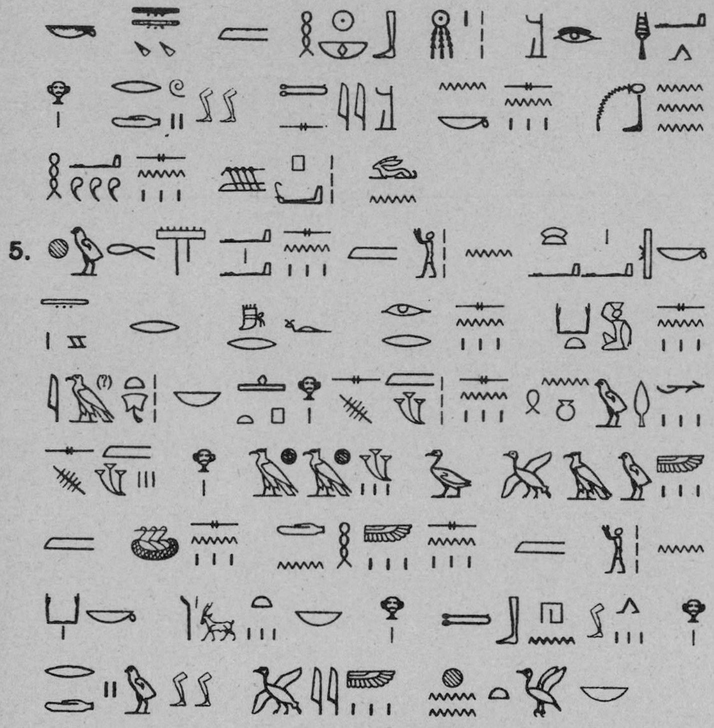

the Two Lands make festival, [men] wake up, stand upon their feet, it is thou who raisest them up. [They] wash their members, they take [their apparel]

5. and array themselves therein, their hands are [stretched out] in praise at thy rising, throughout the land they do their works.

Beasts and cattle of all kinds settle down upon the pastures, shrubs and vegetables flourish, the feathered fowl fly about over their marshes, their feathers praising thy Ka (person). All the cattle rise up on their legs, creatures that fly and insects of all kinds

6. spring into life, when thou risest up on them.

The boats drop down and sail up the river, likewise every road openeth (or showeth itself) at thy rising, the fish in the river swim towards thy face, thy beams are in the depths of the Great Green (*i.e.*, the Mediterranean and Red Seas).

Thou makest offspring to take form in women, creating seed in men. Thou makest the son to live in the womb of his mother, making him to be quiet that he crieth not; thou art a nurse

7. 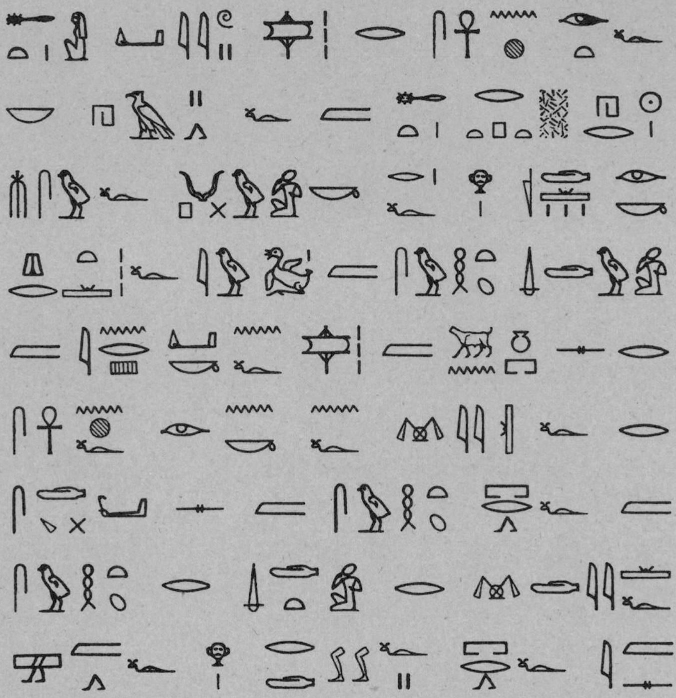

7. in the womb, giving breath to vivify that which he hath made. [When] he droppeth from the womb . . . on the day of his birth [he] openeth his mouth in the [ordinary] manner, thou providest his sustenance.

The young bird in the egg speaketh in the shell, thou givest breath to him inside it to make him to live. Thou makest for him his mature form so that he can crack the shell [being] inside the egg. He cometh forth from the egg, he chirpeṭḥ with all

8.

his might, when he hath come forth from it (the egg), he walketh on his two feet.

O how many are the things which thou hast made!

They are hidden from the face, O thou

8. One God, like whom there is no other. Thou didst create the earth by thy heart (or will), thou alone existing, men and women, cattle, beasts of every kind that are upon the earth, and that move upon feet (or legs), all the creatures that are in the sky and that fly with their wings, [and] the deserts of Syria and Kesh (Nubia), and the Land of Egypt.

Thou settest every person in his place. Thou providest their daily food, every man having the portion allotted to him, [thou] dost compute the duration of his life. Their tongues are different in speech, their characteristics (or forms), and

9. likewise their skins [in colour], giving distinguishing marks to the dwellers in foreign lands.

Thou makest Ḥāpi (the Nile) in the Ṭuat (Underworld), thou bringest it when thou wishest to make mortals to live, inasmuch as thou hast made them for thyself, their Lord who dost support them to

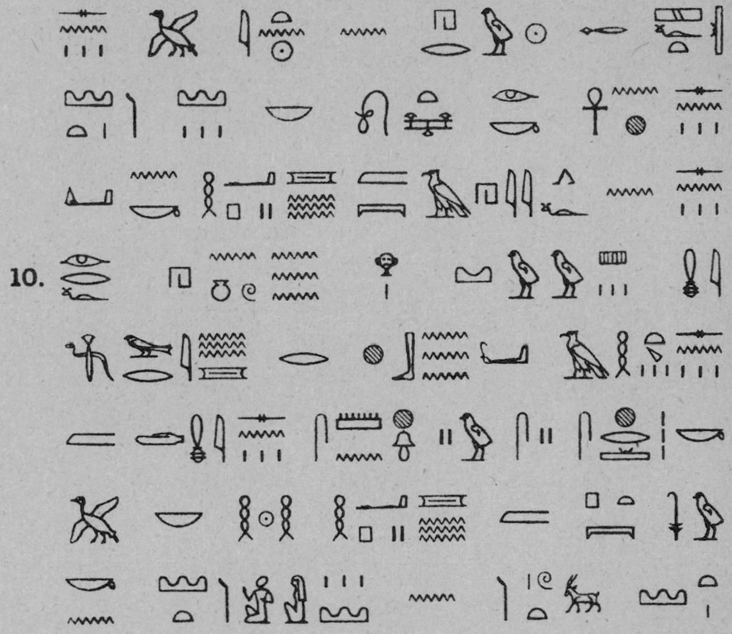

the uttermost, O thou Lord of every land, thou shinest upon them, O ÀTEN of the day, thou great one of majesty.

Thou makest the life of all remote lands. Thou settest a Nile in heaven, which cometh down to them.

10. It maketh a flood on the mountains like the Great Green Sea, it maketh to be watered their fields in their villages. How beneficent are thy plans, O Lord of Eternity! A Nile in heaven art thou for the dwellers in the foreign lands (or deserts), and for all the beasts of the desert that go upon

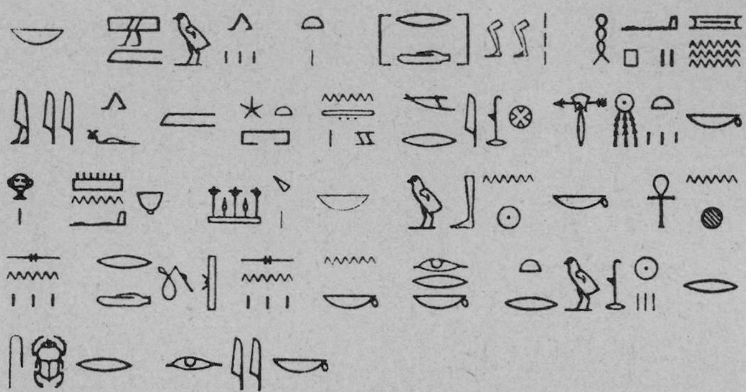

11.

feet (or legs). Ḥāpi (the Nile) cometh from the Ṭuat for the land of Egypt. Thy beams nourish every field; thou risest up [and] they live, they germinate for thee.

Thou makest the Seasons to develop everything that thou hast made:

11 The season of Pert (*i.e.*, Nov. 16–March 16) so that they may refresh themselves, and the season Heh (*i.e.*, March 16–Nov. 16) in order to taste thee.[1] Thou hast made the heaven which is remote that thou mayest shine therein and look upon everything

[1] *I.e.*, for men to feel the heart of Shu who is in the Åten.

12.

that thou hast made. Thy being is one, thou shinest (or, shootest up) among thy creatures as the LIVING ÀTEN, rising, shining, departing afar off, returning. Thou hast made millions of creations (or, evolutions) from thy one self (viz.) towns and cities, villages, fields, roads and river. Every eye (*i.e.*, all men) beholdeth thee confronting it. Thou art the Àten of the day at its zenith.

12. At thy departure thine eye . . . thou didst create their faces so that thou mightest not see. . . . ONE thou didst

13.

make . . . Thou art in my heart. There is no other who knoweth thee except thy son Nefer-kheperu-Rā Uā-en-Rā. Thou hast made him wise to understand thy plans [and] thy power. The earth came into being by thy hand, even as thou hast created them (*i.e.*, men). Thou risest, they live; thou settest, they die. As for thee, there is duration of life in thy members, life is in thee. [All] eyes [gaze upon]

13. thy beauties until thou settest, [when] all labours are relinquished. Thou settest in the West, thou risest, making to flourish . . . for the King. Every man who

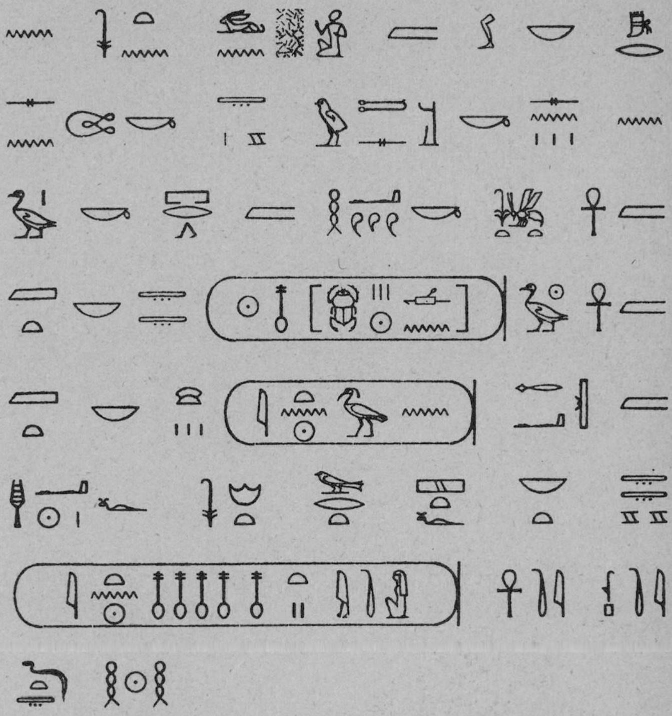

[standeth on his] foot, since thou didst lay the foundation of the earth, thou hast raised up for thy son who came forth from thy body, the King of the South and the North, Living in Truth, Lord of Crowns, Åakhun-Åten, great in the duration of his life [and for] the Royal Wife, great of majesty, Lady of the Two Lands, Nefer-neferu-Åten Nefertiti, living [and] young for ever and ever.

HYMNS TO THE SUN-GOD.

[From the Papyrus of Ani, Sheets 18 and 19.]

The following Hymns are good, typical examples of the songs of praise and thanksgiving which were addressed to the Sun-god by orthodox Egyptians under the XVIIIth dynasty.

A Hymn to Rā when he rises on the Horizon and when he sets in the Land of Life.

Homage to thee, O Rā, who risest as Tem-Ḥeràakhuti.

Thou art adored. Thy beauties are before my eyes, and thy splendour falleth upon my body.

Thou goest to thy setting in the Seqtet Boat with fair winds, and thy heart is glad. The heart of the Māṭet Boat rejoices.

Thou stridest over the heavens in peace, all thy foes being cast down.

The stars which never rest (*i.e.*, the planets) hymn thee, and the stars which never vanish (*i.e.*, the circumpolar stars) glorify thee as thou sinkest to rest in the horizon of Manu.

Thou art beautiful at morn and at eve, O thou Living Lord, the Unchanging One, my Lord.

Homage to thee who risest as Rā and settest as Tem in beauty.

Thou risest and shinest on the back of thy mother [the Sky-goddess], O thou who art crowned king of the gods.

Nut (the Sky-goddess) pays homage to thee, and Maāt (the goddess of Law and Truth) embraces thee at morn and eve.

Joyfully thou stridest over the heavens and the Lake of Testes (a part of heaven) is content thereat. Thine enemy Sebau is cast down headlong, his arms and hands are cut off, and thy dagger has severed the joints of his backbone.

Rā has a fair wind, the Seqtet Boat advances and comes into port.

The gods of the South, the North, the West and the East praise thee, O thou divine substance, from whence all forms of life sprang.

Thou speakest—earth is flooded with silence, O thou ONLY ONE, who didst dwell in heaven before ever the earth and the mountain came into being.

O SHEPHERD, O LORD, O ONLY ONE, Creator of what is, thou didst make the tongue of the Nine Gods. Thou hast made all that sprang from the waters, and thou shootest up from them over the land of the pools of the Lake of Horus.

Let me breathe the air which comes from thy nostrils and the north wind which is from thy mother Nut. Glorify my spirit, O Osiris, make divine my soul.

O Lord of the gods, thou art worshipped at setting in peace, and art exalted because of all thy wondrous works,

Shine thou upon my body each day.

A HYMN TO RĀ WHEN HE RISES IN THE EAST.

Hail, thou Åten, thou lord of rays, who risest on the horizon day by day! Shine thou with thy beams of light upon the face of the Osiris Ani, the truth-speaker, who sings hymns to thee at dawn, and adores thee at eventide. Let his soul appear with thee in heaven. Let him sail out in the Māṭet Boat and arrive in port in the Seqtet Boat, and let him cleave his way among the stars that never vanish.

Homage to thee, O Ḥer-åakhuti, who art Kheperå, the self-created!

When thou risest and sendest forth thy beams upon the lands of the South and the North, thou art beautiful, yea beautiful, and all the gods rejoice when they see thee, the King of Heaven.

Nebt-Unnut (a goddess) is on thy head, her serpents are on thy head, and she takes her place before thee. Thoth stands in the bows of thy boat to destroy thy foes.

The denizens of the Ṭuat (Underworld) come to meet thee, they bow before thee in homage at the sight of thy Beautiful Form.

I would come before thee daily to be with thee and to behold thy Beautiful Åten (Disk). Let me be neither prevented nor repulsed.

Grant that when I look upon thy beauties my members may be made young again, even as are the members of thy favoured ones.

I am one who worshipped thee on earth. Let me enter the Eternal Land in the Everlasting Country. O my Lord, I beseech thee to decree this for me.

Homage to thee who risest as Rā on thy horizon and restest upon Maāt!

Thou passest over the sky, every face watches thy course, thou thyself being unseen. Thou showest thyself at dawn and at eve daily.

The Seqtet Boat of thy Majesty goes forth mightily, thy beams fall upon every face, thy variegated lights and colours cannot be numbered, and cannot be told . . . .

One by thyself alone didst thou come into being from the primeval waters of Nunu (or Nu).

May I go forward as thou dost advance without pause, and dost in a moment pass over untold leagues; and as thou sinkest to rest even so may I.

Thou art crowned with the majesty of thy beauties, thou dost fashion thy members as thou dost advance, and dost produce them without the pangs of labour in the form of Rā, and dost rise up into the heights.

Grant that I may come into the everlasting heaven and the mountain where thy favoured ones dwell. Let me join myself to those who are holy and perfect in the divine Underworld, and let me appear with them to behold thy beauties at eventide. I lift my hands to thee in adoration when thou the living One dost set. Thou art the Eternal Creator and art adored at thy setting in heaven.

I have given my heart to thee without wavering, O thou who art the mightiest of the gods . . .

EGYPTIAN MONOTHEISM.

During the last eighty years the gods of Egypt and the religion of the Ancient Egyptians have been carefully studied by many Egyptologists, but the difficulties which surround these subjects have not yet been cleared away. The responsibility for the existence of these difficulties rests upon the Egyptians themselves, because they did not write books on their religion or explanations of what they believed. But a great many hymns to their gods and legends of their gods and goddesses have come down to us, and from these, thanks to the publication of Egyptian texts during the last thirty years, it is now possible to arrive at a number of important conclusions about the Egyptian religion and its general character. The older Egyptologists debated the question whether it was monotheistic, polytheistic, or pantheistic, and the differences in the opinions which they formed about it will illustrate its difficulty. Champollion believed it to have been "a pure monotheism, which manifested itself externally by a symbolic polytheism."[1] Tiele thought that in the beginning it was polytheistic, but that it developed in two opposite directions; in the one direction gods were multiplied, and in the other it drew nearer and nearer to monotheism.[2] Naville treated it as a "religion of

[1] *L'Égypte*, Paris, 1839, p. 245.

[2] *Geschiedenis van den Godsdienst in de Oudheid*, Amsterdam, 1893, p. 25.

nature, inclining to pantheism."[1] Maspero admitted that the Egyptians applied the epithets, "one God" and "only God" to several gods, even when the god was associated with a goddess and a son, but he adds "ce dieu Un n'était jamais DIEU tout court";[2] the "only god" is the only god Åmen, or the only god Ptaḥ, or the only god Osiris, that is to say, a being determinate possessing a personality, name, attributes, apparel, members, a family, a man infinitely more perfect than men. He is a likeness of the kings of this earth, and his power, like that of all kings, is limited by the power of neighbouring kings. The conception of his unity is geographical and political at least as much as it is religious. Rā, only god of Heliopolis, is not the same as Åmen, only god of Thebes. The Egyptian of Thebes proclaimed the unity of Åmen to the exclusion of Rā, the Egyptian of Heliopolis proclaimed the unity of Rā to the exclusion of Åmen. Each one god, conceived of in this manner, is only the one god of the nome or of the town, and not the one god of the nation recognized as such throughout the country.

On the other hand, de Rougé wrote in 1860, "The unity of a supreme and self-existent being, his eternity, his almightiness, and eternal reproduction as God; the attribution of the creation of the world and of all living beings to this supreme God; the immortality of the soul, completed by the dogma of punishments and rewards; such is the sublime and persistent base which, notwithstanding all deviations and all mythological embellishments, must secure for the beliefs of the Ancient Egyptians a most

[1] *La Religion*, p. 92.
[2] *Histoire Ancienne*, Paris, 1904, p. 33.

honourable place among the religions of antiquity."[1] And in his work on the Religion and Mythology of the Ancient Egyptians[2] Brugsch expressed his conviction that, from the earliest times, a nameless, incomprehensible and eternal God was worshipped by the inhabitants of the Valley of the Nile. This conviction he based on many passages in the religious and moral texts of the Egyptians, in which reference is made to a self-existent almighty Being who seems to be none other than the God of modern nations. From these documents we learn that the Egyptian theologians believed that at one time, which was even to them infinitely remote, nothing existed except a boundless primeval mass of water which was shrouded in darkness, but which contained the ultimate sources of everything that now exists in the universe. In late times this watery mass, which was called Nunu, was regarded as the "Father of the Gods." A something in this water, which formed an essential part of it, felt the desire to create and, having imagined in itself the forms of the beings and things that it intended to create, became operative, and the first creature produced was the god Tem or Kheperȧ, who was the personification of the creative power in the primeval water. This god sent forth from his body Shu (*i.e.*, Heat) and Tefnut (Moisture), and these produced Geb (Earth) and Nut (Sky). Tem or Kheperȧ fashioned the form of everything in his mind and made known his desires to create to his heart, which was personified as Thoth. This god received the creative impulse and invented in his mind a

[1] *Études sur le Rituel Funéraire* (in *Rev. Arch.*, Paris, 1860, p. 12).

[2] *Religion und Mythologie*, Leipzig, 1885, p. 90.

name for the object that was to be created, and when he uttered that name the object came into being. In the texts of the early Dynastic Period Ptaḥ and Khnemu were associated with the god of the primeval water, Nunu or Nu, and they were said to fashion the creatures and things the names of which were pronounced by Thoth. Moreover, they associated the goddess Maāt with Thoth, and the part she played at the creation was very much like that which is attributed to Wisdom in the Book of Proverbs.

What the earliest pictorial forms of Tem, Ptaḥ and Khnemu were is not known, but the first and second appear as men at an early period, and the third is represented by a special form of ram or *kudu*. Rā, who usurped the attributes of Tem, also appears as a man. But of the original creative power which existed of and by itself in the watery mass of Nunu no form is known. The mind of man was incapable of imagining him, and the hand of man was incapable of making a figure that could be considered to be an image or likeness of him. Under the XVIIIth dynasty an Egyptian scribe composed a hymn to Ḥep (or Ḥāp or Ḥāpi), the Nile-god, in which he traced his origin back to the great watery mass of Nunu. He says of him, "He cannot be sculptured in stone in figures whereon is placed the White Crown. He cannot be seen. Service cannot be rendered to him. Gifts cannot be presented to him. He is not to be approached in the sanctuaries. Where he is is not known. He is not to be found in inscribed shrines. No habitation can contain him. There is none who acteṭh as guide to his heart."[1] The

[1] See *Egyptian Hieratic Papyri in the British Museum*, Second Series, London, 1923, pl. LXXIII. (Introduction, p. 31.)

Nile-god is thus described only because he was the direct emanation from the great unseen, unknown and incomprehensible creative power, which had existed for ever and was the source of all created things. Statues of the Nile-god were made under the last dynasties of the New Empire, but the hymn quoted above was written many centuries earlier.

The religious literature of Ancient Egypt of all periods is abundant, yet in no class of it do we find any prayer or petition addressed to this unseen and unknown god. But in the Collections of Moral Aphorisms, or "Teachings," composed by ancient sages, we find several allusions to a divine power to which no personal name is given. The word used to indicate this power is NETER, , or 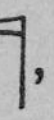, or , or NETHER 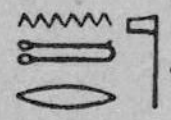. Many have tried to assign a meaning to this word and to find its etymology, but the original meaning of it is at present unknown. The contexts of the passages in which it occurs suggest that it means something like "eternal God." The same word is often used to describe an object, animate or inanimate, which possesses some unusually remarkable power or quality, and in the plural *neteru*, 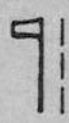, , , , it represents the beings and things to which adoration in one form or another is paid. The great God referred to in the Moral Aphorisms is also spoken of as *pa neter*,  , "the God," just as the Arabs speak of Al-Allâh, *i.e.*, "the Allâh." The following examples drawn from the Precepts of Kagemna

(IVth dynasty) and the Precepts of Ptaḥ-ḥetep (Vth dynasty) will illustrate this use of Neter.[1]

1. The things which God, 𓊹𓏺, doeth cannot be known.

2. Terrify not men. God, 𓊹𓏺, is opposed thereto.

3. The daily bread is under the dispensation of God, 𓊹𓏺.

4. When thou ploughest, labour (?) in the field God, 𓊹𓏺, hath given thee.

5. If thou wouldst be a perfect man make thy son pleasing to God, 𓊹𓏺.

6. God, 𓊹𓏺, loveth obedience; disobedience is hateful to God, 𓊹𓏺.

7. Verily a good (or, beautiful) son is the gift of God, 𓊹𓏺.

These extracts suggest that the writers of the Precepts believed in a God whose plans were inscrutable, who was the feeder of men, who assigned to each a share of the goods of this world, and who expected men to obey his behests and to bring up their children in a way pleasing to him. As time went on the ideas of the Egyptians about God changed, and under the XVIIIth dynasty he lost something of the aloofness with

[1] They are taken from the Prisse Papyrus which was written under the XIth or XIIth dynasty. See Virey, *Études sur le Papyrus Prisse*, Paris, 1877, where a transcript of the hieratic text and a French translation will be found.

which they regarded him, and a fuller idea of his personality existed in their minds. This is clear from the following extracts taken from the Precepts, or Teaching, of Khensu-ḥetep,[1] more generally known as the " Maxims of Ȧni."

1. The God, , magnifies his name.
2. The house of God abominates overmuch speaking. Pray with a loving heart, the words of which are hidden. He will do what is needful for thee, he will hear thy petitions and will accept thine oblations.
3. It is thy God, , who gives thee existence.
4. The God, , is the judge of the truth.
5. When thou makest an offering to thy God beware of offering what he abominates.

The unknown God of the early dynasties has now become a Being who gives men their lives and means of subsistence, who can be approached in a temple, or house, who is pleased with offerings, and with prayers offered up silently to him, and who wishes his name to be magnified. Another extract reads :—

6. " Observe with thine eye his plans (or dispensation). Devote thyself to singing praises to his name. He gives souls to hundreds of thousands of forms. He magnifies him that magnifies him."

[1] See Chabas, *L'Egyptologie, Série I.*, Chalon-sur-Saône, Paris, 1876–78 ; and Amélineau, *La Morale Egyptienne*, Paris, 1892.

The text continues: "Now the god of this earth is Shu, , who is the President of the Horizons. His similitudes are upon the earth, and to them incense and offerings are made daily." Shu in mythological language was the light and heat that emanated from the self-created, self-subsistent and self-existent primeval god, Horus, or Tem, or Kheperȧ. The being who is referred to in the first part of extract No. 6 seems to me to be different from Shu, the god of this earth. And it will be remembered that Ȧmen-ḥetep IV, the "Disk-worshipper," adored "Horus of the Two Horizons in his name of Shu (*i.e.*, Heat) who is in the Ȧten (Disk)."

The Teaching of Ȧmenemȧpt, the son of Kanekht, a work that was probably written under the XVIIIth dynasty, proves quite plainly that the writer distinguished very clearly between God and the gods Rā, the Moon-god, Thoth, Khnem-Rā, Ȧten, etc. In the following extracts he clearly refers to God.

1. Leave the angry man in the hands of God . . . . God knows how to requite him (Col. V).
2. Carry not away the servant of the God for the benefit of another (Col. VI).
3. Take good heed to Nebertcher, 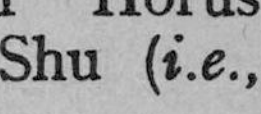 (Lord of the Universe) (Col. VIII).
4. Though a man's tongue steers the boat, it is Nebertcher who is the pilot (Col. XIX).
5. Truth is the great porter (or bearer) of God (Col. XXI).
6. Seat thyself in the hands of God (Col. XXIII).

7. A man prepares the straw for his building, but God is his architect.

   It is he who throws down, it is he who builds up daily.

   It is he who makes a man to arrive in Amentt (the Other World) [where] he is safe in the hand of God (Col. XXIV).

8. The love of God, praised and adored be he! is more than the respect of the Chief (Col. XXVI).[1]

It will be noted that in none of these extracts is any attempt made to describe God, *Neter*, and that he is never called "One," or "Only One." The truth is that the Egyptians felt that they could not describe him and that they knew nothing about him, except that he existed. This great nameless, unseen and unknown God handed over to a number of inferior beings the direction and management of heaven and earth and everything which was in them. Those that were kind and considerate to the human race men called gods, and those that were malevolent and inimical they called devils. Each community or village, however small, possessed its own "god," whose power and importance depended upon the wealth and social position of his worshippers. But the Egyptian, whilst adoring the "god," *Neter*, of his native city, was ready to admit the existence of another *Neter*, who was probably the Being whom we call God. Thus, in Chapter CXXV of the Book of the Dead, the deceased says in his declaration before the Forty-two gods, "I have not cursed God,"

[1] See *Egyptian Hieratic Papyri*, ed. Budge, Second Series, London, 1923.

, and "I have not contemned the god of my city,  .[1] The distinction between "God" and "god of the city" was quite clear in the mind of the Egyptian.

It has been claimed by some that Åmenḥetep IV was the first monotheist in Egypt, but the acceptance of this statement depends upon what meaning is given to the word monotheism, *i.e.*, the doctrine of there being only one god. The passages from the Moral Papyri quoted above show that the Egyptian priests and learned men were monotheistic, even though they do not proclaim the oneness of the god to whom they refer. The idea of oneness was well understood under the Ancient Empire, but in the Pyramid Texts the attribute is ascribed to the "gods" and to kings as well as to God. Thus in Tetȧ (l. 237) the "lord one" 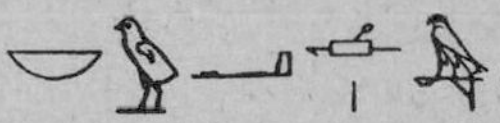, is mentioned; in Merenrā I the king is called "great god alone," 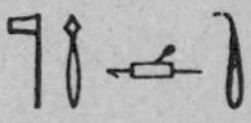 (l. 127),[2] and is said to be stronger than every god; and in Pepi II (l. 952) the king is called the "one of heaven," 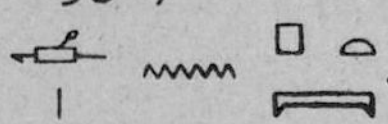. Now the monotheism of Åmenḥetep IV was different from that of the writers of the Moral Papyri, and the oneness of Åten which he proclaimed resembled the oneness of several other Egyptian solar gods and also

[1] From the Papyrus of Nebseni. Early XVIIIth dynasty.

[2] And "Lord of the earth to its limit" 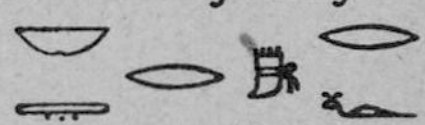 (l. 128).

gods to whom solar attributes had not been originally ascribed. Tem, Horus of the Two Horizons, and Rā, each of these is called "One," and "only one," whether mentioned singly or together as a triad, and the same title was given to Åmen after his fusion with Rā. And whilst Åmenḥetep IV was proclaiming the oneness of Åten in the city of Åten, the worshipper of Åmen was proclaiming the oneness of Åmen in Thebes, the worshipper of Rā or Tem was proclaiming the oneness of his god in Heliopolis, and so on throughout the country. And it is interesting to note that votaries of Neith of Saïs proclaimed that their goddess was "One," 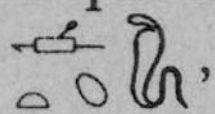,[1] that she first created herself and then produced Rā from her own body. The second portion of a fine Hymn to the solar triad, which is preserved in the Papyrus of Ani (sheet 19), and is addressed to Rā-Tem-Heråakhuti the "only one," adds Osiris to this "only one" thus: "Praise be to thee, O Osiris, eternal Lord, Un-nefer, Heråakhuti, whose forms are manifold and whose attributes are majestic, Ptaḥ-Seker-Tem in Ånu, lord of the hidden shrine and creator of Ḥetkaptaḥ (Memphis) . . . thou turnest thy face to the Other World, thou makest the earth to shine like *tchām* (gilded copper?). The dead rise up to look at thee, they breathe the air and they see thy face like that of the Åten (Disk) when he rises on his horizon. Since they see thee their hearts are content, O thou who art Eternity and Everlastingness."

It is impossible for Åmenḥetep IV to have indulged in the philosophical speculations as to the unity of God, with which he is sometimes credited, but which were only evolved by the Greek

[1] See Budge, *Gods of the Egyptians*, Vol. I, p. 458.

philosophers a thousand years later. It is, however, very probable that he wished Àten, as the god of absolute truth and justice, to become the national god of Egypt and divine ruler of all the countries of the Sûdân and Western Asia that formed his dominions. If that be so, he was born too late to bring this about, even supposing that he was physically and mentally fit to undertake such a task. When he ascended the throne, Àmen, or Àmen-Rā, the King of the Gods, the Lord of the world, was actually what Àmenḥetep wished Àten to be. Àmen had expelled the Hyksos and set the first king of the XVIIIth dynasty upon his throne, and he had given victory to the successors of Àāḥmes I and filled Egypt with the wealth of the Sûdân and Western Asia. Àmen had become the overlord of the gods, and his fame filled the greater part of the world that was known to the Egyptians. It was impossible to overthrow the great and wealthy priesthood of Àmen, to say nothing of the social institutions of which Àmen was the head. The monotheism of Àmenḥetep from a religious point of view was not new, but from a political point of view it was. It consisted chiefly of the dogma that Àmen was unfit to be the national god of Egypt, the Sûdân and Syria, and that Àten was more just, more righteous, and more merciful than the upstart god of Thebes, and that Àten alone was fitted to be the national god of Egypt and her dominions. When Àmenḥetep tried to give a practical form to his views, his attempt was accompanied, as has frequently been the case with religious "reformers," by the confiscation of sacrosanct property, and by social confusion and misery. It was fortunate for Egypt that she only produced one king who was an individualist and idealist, a pacifist and a religious "reformer" all in one.

Âmenḥetep IV attempted to establish a *positive* religion, and as a religious innovator he spoke and acted as if he were divinely inspired and had a divine revelation to give to men, and in every way he tried to depart from the traditions of the past. He never realised that if his religion was to take root and flourish it must be in contact all along the line with the older ideas and practices which he found among his people. Religion did not begin with him in Egypt. He failed in his self-appointed task because his religion did not appeal to the tradition and religious instincts and susceptibilities that already existed among the Egyptians, and because he would not tolerate the traditional forms in which their spiritual feelings were embodied.

Variegated glass bottle in the form of a fish.
From Tall al-'Amârnah. British Museum, No. 55193.
[Presented by the Egypt Exploration Society, 1921.]

INDEX.